SUPERNATURAL AND PHILOSOPHY

The Blackwell Philosophy and PopCulture Series
Series editor William Irwin

A spoonful of sugar helps the medicine go down, and a healthy helping of popular culture clears the cobwebs from Kant. Philosophy has had a public relations problem for a few centuries now. This series aims to change that, showing that philosophy is relevant to your life—and not just for answering the big questions like "To be or not to be?" but for answering the little questions: "To watch or not to watch *South Park*?" Thinking deeply about TV, movies, and music doesn't make you a "complete idiot." In fact it might make you a philosopher, someone who believes the unexamined life is not worth living and the unexamined cartoon is not worth watching.

Already published in the series:

24 and Philosophy: The World According to Jack
Edited by Jennifer Hart Weed, Richard Brian Davis, and Ronald Weed

30 Rock and Philosophy: We Want to Go to There
Edited by J. Jeremy Wisnewski

Alice in Wonderland and Philosophy: Curiouser and Curiouser
Edited by Richard Brian Davis

Arrested Development and Philosophy: They've Made a Huge Mistake
Edited by Kristopher Phillips and J. Jeremy Wisnewski

The Avengers and Philosophy: Earth's Mightiest Thinkers
Edited by Mark D. White

Batman and Philosophy: The Dark Knight of the Soul
Edited by Mark D. White and Robert Arp

Battlestar Galactica and Philosophy: Knowledge Here Begins Out There
Edited by Jason T. Eberl

The Big Bang Theory and Philosophy: Rock, Paper, Scissors, Aristotle, Locke
Edited by Dean Kowalski

The Big Lebowski and Philosophy: Keeping Your Mind Limber with Abiding Wisdom
Edited by Peter S. Fosl

Black Sabbath and Philosophy: Mastering Reality
Edited by William Irwin

The Daily Show and Philosophy: Moments of Zen in the Art of Fake News
Edited by Jason Holt

Downton Abbey and Philosophy: The Truth Is Neither Here Nor There
Edited by Mark D. White

Ender's Game and Philosophy: The Logic Gate is Down
Edited by Kevin S. Decker

Family Guy and Philosophy: A Cure for the Petarded
Edited by J. Jeremy Wisnewski

Final Fantasy and Philosophy: The Ultimate Walkthrough
Edited by Jason P. Blahuta and Michel S. Beaulieu

Game of Thrones and Philosophy: Logic Cuts Deeper Than Swords
Edited by Henry Jacoby

The Girl With the Dragon Tattoo and Philosophy: Everything is Fire
Edited by Eric Bronson

Green Lantern and Philosophy: No Evil Shall Escape this Book
Edited by Jane Dryden and Mark D. White

Heroes and Philosophy: Buy the Book, Save the World
Edited by David Kyle Johnson

The Hobbit and Philosophy: For When You've Lost Your Dwarves, Your Wizard, and Your Way
Edited by Gregory Bassham and Eric Bronson

House and Philosophy: Everybody Lies
Edited by Henry Jacoby

The Hunger Games and Philosophy: A Critique of Pure Treason
Edited by George Dunn and Nicolas Michaud

Inception and Philosophy: Because It's Never Just a Dream
Edited by David Johnson

Iron Man and Philosophy: Facing the Stark Reality
Edited by Mark D. White

Lost and Philosophy: The Island Has Its Reasons
Edited by Sharon M. Kaye

Mad Men and Philosophy: Nothing Is as It Seems
Edited by James South and Rod Carveth

Metallica and Philosophy: A Crash Course in Brain Surgery
Edited by William Irwin

The Office and Philosophy: Scenes from the Unfinished Life
Edited by J. Jeremy Wisnewski

Sons of Anarchy and Philosophy
Edited by George A. Dunn and Jason T. Eberl

South Park and Philosophy: You Know, I Learned Something Today
Edited by Robert Arp

Spider-Man and Philosophy: The Web of Inquiry
Edited by Jonathan Sanford

Superman and Philosophy: What Would the Man of Steel Do?
Edited by Mark D. White

Supernatural and Philosophy: Metaphysics and Monsters … for Idjits
Edited by Galen A. Foresman

Terminator and Philosophy: I'll Be Back, Therefore I Am
Edited by Richard Brown and Kevin S. Decker

True Blood and Philosophy: We Wanna Think Bad Things with You
Edited by George Dunn and Rebecca Housel

Twilight and Philosophy: Vampires, Vegetarians, and the Pursuit of Immortality
Edited by Rebecca Housel and J. Jeremy Wisnewski

The Ultimate Daily Show and Philosophy: More Moments of Zen, More Moments of Indecision Theory
Edited by Jason Holt

The Ultimate Harry Potter and Philosophy: Hogwarts for Muggles
Edited by Gregory Bassham

The Ultimate Lost and Philosophy: Think Together, Die Alone
Edited by Sharon Kaye

The Ultimate South Park and Philosophy: Respect My Philosophah!
Edited by Robert Arp and Kevin S. Decker

The Walking Dead and Philosophy: Shotgun. Machete. Reason.
Edited by Christopher Robichaud

Watchmen and Philosophy: A Rorschach Test
Edited by Mark D. White

X-Men and Philosophy: Astonishing Insight and Uncanny Argument in the Mutant X-Verse
Edited by Rebecca Housel and J. Jeremy Wisnewski

SUPERNATURAL
AND
PHILOSOPHY

METAPHYSICS
AND MONSTERS ...
FOR IDJITS

Edited By Galen A. Foresman

WILEY Blackwell

This edition first published 2013
© 2013 John Wiley & Sons, Inc.

Registered Office
John Wiley & Sons, Ltd, The Atrium, Southern Gate, Chichester, West Sussex, PO19 8SQ, UK

Editorial Offices
350 Main Street, Malden, MA 02148-5020, USA
9600 Garsington Road, Oxford, OX4 2DQ, UK
The Atrium, Southern Gate, Chichester, West Sussex, PO19 8SQ, UK

For details of our global editorial offices, for customer services, and for information about how
to apply for permission to reuse the copyright material in this book please see our website at
www.wiley.com/wiley-blackwell.

The right of Galen A. Foresman to be identified as the author of the editorial material in this work
has been asserted in accordance with the UK Copyright, Designs and Patents Act 1988.

Library of Congress Cataloging-in-Publication Data

Supernatural and philosophy : metaphysics and monsters for idjits / edited by Galen A. Foresman.
    pages   cm. – (The Blackwell philosophy and pop culture series)
  Includes bibliographical references and index.
  ISBN 978-1-118-61595-9 (pbk. : alk. paper)
  1. Supernatural (Television program : 2005–)   I. Foresman, Galen A., editor of compilation.
  PN1992.77.S84S87 2013
  791.45'72–dc23
                                        2013017489

A catalogue record for this book is available from the British Library.

Cover image: Sky and lightning © sankai/iStockphoto; House © Shaun Lowe/Getty Images;
Chevrolet Impala 1969 © schlol/iStockphoto.
Cover design by www.simonlevy.co.uk

Set in 10.5/13pt Sabon by SPi Publisher Services, Pondicherry, India

1   2013

Contents

Acknowledgments

I would be remiss if I didn't begin the acknowledgments by recognizing the dedicated fans of the show, many of whom began their stalwart fandom during an ancient time when people watched shows on large boxy televisions at specific times during the week to the exclusion of other programming. These fans made true sacrifices with their time and attention, helping to make *Supernatural* the success it is today. For all those fans, as well as those who have joined them along the way, I am very grateful.

Many thanks are owed to Jeff Dean for helping get this book off the ground and for his steady oversight in keeping it there. However, much of the thanks for guidance and timeliness belong to Bill Irwin, whose remarkably short correspondences always gave me several hours of material to think upon, not unlike the late great Bobby Singer. Additionally, Robert Arp was instrumental in putting this book together, providing Castiel-like guidance and moral support whenever he was summoned. Thanks to Lindsay Bourgeois for cheerfully responding to all my inane questions and requests, as well as to Jennifer Bray for her help wading through arcane rules from ancient tombs of U.S. law and other clearance-related mystical rituals. Thanks also to Louise Spencely for swiftly copy-editing and laying waste to my many double-spaces.

My dear friend and colleague, Karen Hornsby, was enormously helpful in keeping extra work off my plate during much of the editing of this book. She's a tireless Dean Winchester.

Most importantly, none of the work I put into this book would have been remotely possible without the loving patience and encouragement of my wife, Amy. I'd be just another John Winchester without her, and I thank her especially for working tirelessly to care for our brood, so that I could geek out on my favorite show for hours and hours at a time.

Introduction
Codename: GhostPhacers

[From a drive adjacent the myriad of external drives of Ed Zeddmore and Harry Spengler ...]

When Alan J. Corbett died courageously seeking truth, we knew our quest was only just beginning. Spurred by the loss of our brave intern and cook, we GhostFacers have rededicated our lives to fulfilling the mission Corbett was slain so admirably pursuing, opening "people's eyes to the truth: that ghosts do, in fact, exist," along with many other things that do, in fact, also exist along with ghosts.

Now surely you're wondering why the GhostFacers are working under the auspices of *Supernatural and Philosophy*, and no doubt you're rightfully concerned about the degree of douchnozzelian chicanery that has coerced our hand in adopting such a title for our manifesto of truth, as opposed to the very razor *GhostFacer Manifesto*. As we have said secretly elsewhere at our website:

> The GhostFacers are poised to take a number of different industries by storm. These industries include: science, math, philosophy, religion, agriculture, government and entertainment with the potential of affecting some major public works projects as well. In fact, it is safe to say that there is no aspect of human civilization that will not be impacted to some degree by GhostFacers.

Supernatural and Philosophy: Metaphysics and Monsters ... for Idjits, First Edition.
Edited by Galen A. Foresman.
© 2013 John Wiley & Sons, Inc. Published 2013 by John Wiley & Sons, Inc.

So fear not, for we're simply taking our first steps in the larger plan to subvert these many different industries. All of this requires working covertly and duplicitously to bring you what those two wanted criminals—the Wine-chesters—won't: insight into the greatest mysteriosities humankind has ever known. To that end, we have begun here by subverting the very foundations of all the industries mentioned previously and some that went unmentioned. We do this through the mystery that is philosophy.

Recent extensive research utilizing the power of the interwebs through the "Search the Web" web-based search engine reveals that the first ten results of the word, "philosophy," are all websites. From this we've deduced that philosophy is more popular than we first expected, and infiltrating it won't be the cake-walk in the park that we originally believed it to be. After consulting a research librarian from the special reference section of a non-descript college in Wilkes-Barre, PA, we have confirmed that the word "philo-sophy" has ancient roots in the Greek word philosophia (φιλοσοφία), which means something like "loving wisdom" or "loving know-ledge." Regardless of the exact meaning, we're confident that this was an important and powerful secret, although it left unexplained why the ten websites we looked at had nothing to do with loving anything, even despite our disabling "safe-search."

Armed now with knowledge, we used secret contacts to recruit experts in this industry of philosophy, all bona fide, card-carrying wisdom lovers. And just to be clear, I should say that by "we" I have so far meant, me, alone, like a wolf with no pack that was trying to organize a pack of wolves together via email and other means. I was a wolf howling in search of other wolves, and after the howl of my call went out, there was a chorus of howling replies. Amidst that choir of howling, philosophers the world over taught me many secrets about what we truly know and don't know. Philosophers who readily admitted that they knew nothing, but continued nevertheless to love and pursue this fictional thing they claimed not to know. When I inquired as to whether knowledge was some sort of tulpa, I was rebuked for speaking blasphemy.

After meticulously transcribing these dialogues onto ancient papyrus scrolls, I made a sandwich and a ring of salt. Placing the scrolls securely within a duffle bag, I climbed safely inside—the ring of salt, not the duffle bag. Equipped now with time, sustenance, and the safety that only a ring of salt and a duffle bag can provide, I began to read. And the more I read, the more my eyes were opened to a world I did not fully understand. From my original call on philosophers, my recruits were legion, but only the strongest and finest were permitted to remain in this elite ghost-facing wolf pack of wisdom lovers, and so a multitude of scrolls were committed to the flames.

Finally, I should point out that although I'm not an original member of the GhostFacers, I suppose you could technically consider me an honorary co-founder who's not, yet, officially recognized as having any founding role or leadership role or other role, with the core team. But my recent contributions to the Mission are, without a doubt, somewhat noteworthy, hence my strong hunch that I'll hear an update regarding my membership to the team soon. Having said that, I can confirm for you, dear reader, that I have heard from a good source that says my resume may have been received by the visionary leader Ed Zeddmore himself and/or co-founder and tactical expert, Harry Spangler. In either case, it is certain to probably mean that my unofficial and unrecognized honorary co-founder status is soon to convert to at least either "officially unrecognized" or "unofficially recognized." Therefore, I speak with some authority when I say that this collection of essays is comprised of the most mind-blowing, eye-popping, soul-exploding revelations—nay, revolutions!—in truth and wisdom loving.

So tether your brain, don safety-tested safety goggles, and prepare for the imminent detonation of your soul, because in reading these pages you have unofficially joined the yet-to-be-recognized movement in the philosophy of ghost-facing, henceforth codenamed, "GhostPhacing." (The "Ph" is for Philosophy!)

Part One

OF MONSTERS AND MORALS

Part One

CHARACTERS AND
SYMBOLS

Chapter 1

Are Monsters Members of the Moral Community?

Nathan Stout

SAM:	How do you do it? How does Dad do it?
DEAN:	Well for one, them. I figure our family's so screwed to Hell maybe we can help some others. Makes things a little bit more bearable. I'll tell you what else helps. *Killing as many evil sons of bitches as I possibly can.*

In this exchange between Sam and Dean from the Season 1 episode "Wendigo," Dean establishes the attitude that the brothers will take toward the things they hunt. Monsters are evil and harmful to others, so the brothers are completely justified in eliminating the various creatures they encounter. The viewer finds herself pulling for Sam and Dean to succeed, to safely avert the Apocalypse, to put the vengeful spirit to rest, to exorcise the demon, and, in many cases, to kill the monster, but monsters often present a formidable challenge for our view of the brothers' moral character. Not only do we care about the safety and well-being of the protagonists, but we also care about the morality of their actions. We want the good guys to win, but we also want them to be *good* guys.

In this sense, *Supernatural* presents us with a difficult puzzle. We find ourselves holding contradictory attitudes about Sam and Dean. We want them to save those who are in danger, but we have a difficult time squaring this desire with our concern that they act morally. What if that monster doesn't deserve to be killed? What if

Supernatural and Philosophy: Metaphysics and Monsters ... for Idjits, First Edition.
Edited by Galen A. Foresman.
© 2013 John Wiley & Sons, Inc. Published 2013 by John Wiley & Sons, Inc.

the monster is not responsible for his or her actions? What if the monster's actions are justified, or, at the very least, excusable? In short, what if that monster is really a lot like you and me, a genuine member of the moral community?

Moral Community? Is That Like a Coven?

Moral philosophy is concerned with matters of right and wrong, and with answering questions about how we should live. Moral philosophy aims to tell us how to think about particular moral dilemmas; it aims to give us principles by which we can make moral decisions; and it aims to give us insight into how those moral principles are grounded. In doing all of this, moral philosophy should also help us to determine precisely whom, or what, we should consider when making moral decisions. In other words, moral philosophy should be able to tell us which creatures deserve moral consideration, which beings we must take into account when deciding which actions are right and which actions are wrong.

By telling us these things, moral philosophy sets boundaries on what philosophers refer to as the "moral community." In essence, to be a member of the moral community is to be the type of being that deserves moral consideration from others. For example, most people believe that it is wrong to kill another human being just for the fun of it. The reason we feel this way is because humans are members of the moral community. The fact that you are a member of the moral community means that you can't be killed for the fun of it. In any moral decision that we make, we must take into account the effects that it might have for members of the moral community.

So how do we know who or what belongs to the moral community? One way that philosophers have gone about defining the boundaries of the moral community is by paying special attention to the notion of moral responsibility. In other words, they have attempted to define the moral community as the group of individuals who are capable of being held responsible for their actions.

In his essay, "Freedom and Resentment," P.F. Strawson argues that we ought to understand moral responsibility as being tied to the "reactive attitudes."[1] Reactive attitudes are emotions that we experience in response to another's actions toward us; some of these emotions—such as resentment or indignation—are of an overtly moral nature. Therefore, it is best to understand moral responsibility as applying only to those beings that are the *appropriate* target of these moral emotions. For example, when a toddler uses a living room wall as a canvas for her finger-paint masterpiece, it might be *appropriate* to feel frustration toward her, but surely, it would *not be appropriate* to resent the child for her actions. We would say that the person who is morally outraged at the toddler's behavior is overreacting. Children are different from fully developed adults who should know better. Thus, the appropriateness or inappropriateness of a moralized attitude ought to give us insight into the moral status of the creature toward which we hold the attitude.

For Strawson, there are two factors that might render a moral emotion inappropriate: how much control you have of your actions and the type of thing you are. For example, in "Asylum," Sam shoots Dean in the chest with a shotgun full of rock salt while under the control of the spirit of Dr. Ellicott. Since Sam's actions aren't under his control, Dean shouldn't be *angry* with him. After all, it wasn't really Sam's fault. It was Dr. Ellicott's spirit. Sometimes, however, a creature can be perfectly in control of its actions, and yet, because of the type of thing it is, we cannot appropriately feel moral emotions toward it. Consider Sam's character navigating life without the benefit of having a soul throughout most of Season 6. Assuming a popular understanding of the soul, which says a soul is necessary to act morally, we ought to consider Sam in a much different light as far as moral responsibility is concerned. In Season 6, Sam is simply not the type of creature toward which it is appropriate to hold the moral attitudes. Being angry with Sam in this situation is like being angry with a robot. We ought to consider him with what Strawson calls an "objectivity of attitude." He is a being whom we must manage or control; such beings are unable to enter into normal moral relationships wherein the moral emotions have a place. As a result, we must treat them objectively, as if they were an "object of social policy."

How can we tell when a creature is the sort of thing that is the appropriate target for moral emotions? One promising approach makes an individual the appropriate target of moral emotions only if the being has the ability to understand and be motivated by moral reasons. In other words, the being must be able to understand when a situation presents her with a duty to act in a certain way, and the recognition of this fact must motivate her to fulfill that duty.

Monsters and the Moral Community: Group 1–Low-Functioning Monsters

Sam and Dean have a veritable trophy case of monster hunts. They have killed everything from your run-of-the-mill werewolves, vampires, and shapeshifters to more exotic creatures such as shtrigas, wraiths, and djinn. Thus, it will be helpful to begin placing these creatures into different categories based on our intuitions about their status as members of the moral community. Doing this allows us to distinguish those monsters that are firmly outside the boundaries of the moral community, thereby highlighting the hard cases, wherein moral status is more difficult to determine.

In "Heart" Dean sums up our first group, low-functioning monsters, saying, "What about a human by day, freak, animal, killing-machine by moonlight don't you understand?" These monsters obviously fall outside of the moral community. They kill humans out of a basic instinct. Their mental abilities are no more advanced than a wild animal, and, thus, they show no ability to understand or be motivated by moral reasons. For this reason, it would be absurd to criticize them for acting immorally. For example, if my dog rummages through the garbage at night making a huge mess in the house, it would make sense for me to be angry and say, "Bad dog!" It wouldn't, however, make sense for me to feel offended and say, "How dare you treat my home with such disrespect!"

One excellent example of a low-functioning monster comes to us in the second episode of Season 1, "Wendigo." A wendigo is a creature that hunts humans for food. They actually begin life as human beings and become monsters when they turn to cannibalism for survival after being stranded in the wilderness. If enough human flesh is consumed, "over years, [the cannibal] becomes this less than human thing ... always hungry." The wendigo, then, is an example of an animal-like monster. It is a skilled hunter, but its skill is a product of its instincts. It does not have the normal human emotional capacities. Instead, it is driven by self-preservation and its need to feed.

Another enlightening example of a low-functioning monster is the werewolf. In the episode "Heart," Sam and Dean encounter a woman named Madison, who turns out to be a werewolf. As noted before, Dean describes them as "freak, animal, killing-machines." While in their werewolf state, these monsters are driven by base, animal instincts. Later in the episode, Sam exhorts Dean to refrain from killing Madison, saying, "Maybe she really doesn't know she's changing, you know? Maybe when the creature takes over she blacks out ... What if some animal part of her brain saw both of those guys [the murder victims] as threats?" Sam is pointing out how were-wolves pose an interesting moral question for us, which we will come back to. For now it seems clear that while they are in their wolf-state, these creatures are not members of the moral community.

Group 2–Antisocial Monsters

In addition to the Group 1 monsters, there is another set of crea-tures that falls clearly outside of the boundaries of the moral community. These are the "antisocial monsters." Such creatures share distinct similarities with individuals who are diagnosed with various forms of antisocial personality disorder, which is typically characterized by an inability to feel empathy and regard for the rights of others, appearing manipulative and lacking in conscience. Monsters from this category fall outside of the moral community as well, albeit in a very different way.

Demons provide a good illustration of antisocial monsters. Throughout the series, demons are portrayed as purely evil, wantonly killing human beings and engaging in torture for fun. Unlike the Group 1 monsters, however, they have highly developed mental abilities. They rely on reasoning to plan and achieve their goals and, by all accounts, they appear to be equal to human beings in terms of mental prowess.

Similarly, leviathans are prototypical antisocial monsters. They lack any regard for the human race and implement a plan to turn us into a factory-farm-style food supply. Leviathans show a high degree of intelligence, and they are clearly able to conceive of and execute elaborate plans for the sake of achieving a rational goal, which is ultimately what precludes them from being classified among the Group 1 monsters.

Why shouldn't we consider Group 2 monsters full members of the moral community, and simply hold them morally responsible for their actions? The answer, I think, lies in their inability to recognize moral reasons. Demons, for example, are *purely* evil and simply cannot understand a moral demand made by a human. Suppose that instead of making plans to kill Lilith in order to avert the Apocalypse, Sam and Dean decided that they should explain to her that she has a moral obligation to avoid destroying humanity. Obviously, we could expect Lilith to make short work of the brothers and continue on her quest to destroy humanity. But why is this so obvious?

The reason seems to be that she is incapable of understanding a moral reason with respect to humans. She may very well be aware that human beings live according to a moral code, but she certainly wouldn't care in the least about it. It simply wouldn't motivate her, and this motivational component is part of what it means to be a member of the moral community. The same explanation could be given with respect to the leviathans. They simply aren't moved by moral reasons, thus precluding them from being members of the moral community and thereby excluding them as appropriate targets of the moral emotions.

Group 3–The Moral Monsters

For any creature to be a member of the moral community it must care about and be motivated by moral reasons. Moral reasons don't register as important decision-making factors for either

Group 1 or Group 2 monsters. But there are some monsters that do seem to take moral reasons into consideration when they make decisions, and because of this, we should include them in the moral community. These are the Group 3 monsters, and they pose a particularly interesting challenge to the moral character of Sam and Dean.

In "Bloodlust," Sam and Dean are hunting vampires in Montana. Unlike other vampires the brothers have encountered, these ones do not feed on human blood. Instead, they have learned to survive by consuming the blood of cows. Their reasons for not killing humans are to spare humans from suffering and to help their vampire species survive undetected.

These vampires give us reason to believe that vampires are indeed members of the moral community. The fact that these vampires refrain from killing humans signifies that they are motivated by moral reasons. It would, therefore, be entirely appropriate for the brothers to hold the various reactive attitudes toward them. This is a running theme in the vampire-based episodes of *Supernatural*. In "Dead Man's Blood," the vampire Luther pleads with John Winchester, "Why can't you leave us alone? We have as much *right* to live as you do." Again, in "Fresh Blood," we encounter a vampire who claims that "hunters slaughtered my entire nest like they were having a party, *murdered* my daughter." The notion of having a right to live and the concept of murder (defined as *wrongful* killing) both have moral elements to them, and the fact that these monsters understand this suggests a sensitivity to moral reasoning.

This realization is very important for how we view Sam and Dean. When Sam tells Dean that the vampires are not killing people, Dean responds by saying, "What part of 'vampires' don't you understand, Sam? If it's supernatural, we kill it, end of story. That's our job ... They're all the same, Sam. They're not human, okay? We have to exterminate every last one of them." Here Dean sounds extraordinarily bigoted and close-minded. But by the end of the episode, Dean's attitude has changed. He tells Sam, "I wish we never took this job. It just jacked everything up ... What if we killed things that didn't deserve killing?" Dean seems to be coming to the conclusion that monsters are not categorically evil, that some might actually deserve moral consideration. This realization by Dean—for better or worse—makes a huge difference in our opinion of his character. After all, it's hard to root for a bigoted jack-ass.

Unfortunately, in "The Girl Next Door," we are introduced to another Group 3 monster that Dean handles differently. Sam begins investigating a string of murders involving unsavory individuals. The case is similar to one that the family had when Sam was a child, in which he unknowingly befriended a kitsune, named Amy. Kitsune are creatures that require human pituitary glands in order to survive. Amy and her son have been surviving on the glands of dead people she obtains through her job as a mortician. Gross to be sure, but it isn't like she's killing anyone. Only recently has she begun killing a few not-so-great people to save her sick child. Sam exhorts Dean, once again, to spare the life of this monster. And though Dean at first listens to his brother, he later kills Amy anyway without Sam knowing.

Amy, the kitsune, is clearly a member of the moral community, and it is for this very reason that we feel anger or outrage at Dean for killing her. He has reverted to his old understanding of what it is to be a monster. He tells Amy before killing her, "[People] are who they are. No matter how hard you try, you are who you are. You will kill again." Rather than using the lesson learned from Lenore and other vampires, Dean once again takes up the if-it's-supernatural-kill-it attitude, and the viewer finds this objectionable precisely because Amy is an example of a moral monster, a card-carrying member of the moral community.

Good Guys?

Being a member of the moral community means being capable of understanding and caring about moral obligations, but there is another side of the coin. It also means that all members of the moral community have moral obligations to one another. That is not to say that members of the moral community may *never* be killed. Self-defense, for example, can be a justifiable reason to kill another member of the moral community. Sam and Dean act morally when they kill moral monsters in self-defense or to protect the lives of others.

Sam and Dean are admirable for their consistent dedication to helping save the lives of other people, but this seems inconsistent with their apparent disregard for the lives of the moral monsters they hunt, which should leave us questioning whether or not Sam and Dean are really good.

Suppose I must kill someone to save your life, because they are threatening to kill you. If after taking the person's life I popped open a cooler, leaned up against my '67 Chevy, and took a long swig of beer as the sun set, then you might think I'm cold and callous. After all, I've just killed another member of the moral community as though it were just any other job. I suppose that would make sense if I was an executioner, but it would be sociopathic of me to think I was just a hunter, doing what we do. At the end of the day, killing a member of the moral community ought to weigh heavily on us, and we ought to expect the brothers to feel the gravity of this after they kill a monster. Believing this isn't some sort of naïve sympathy for the devil. When Sam and Dean kill with no remorse, our good guys aren't really as good as we think.

Note

1. P.F. Strawson, "Freedom and Resentment," in Gary Watson ed., *Free Will*, 2nd edn (New York: Oxford University Press, 2003), 72–93.

Chapter 2

Aristotle's Metaphysics of Monsters and Why We Love *Supernatural*

Galen A. Foresman and Francis Tobienne, Jr.

Sam and Dean hunt monsters, and monsters are pretty freaky. No doubt, some people are pretty freaky too, but monsters are unique in that they possess an element of shock and mystery that people do not. If Sam and Dean were vigilantes hunting down run-of-the-mill bad guys, would you bother watching the show? I'm willing to bet that there's something about the way monsters freak you out that compels you to watch Sam and Dean hunt them.

When children use the word "monster," they do so in the very normal dictionary sense, referring to creatures that are large, ugly, and frightening. To speak of a "cute monster," "comforting monster," or even "little monster" is oxymoronic, like "jumbo shrimp." Children actually know this, which is why they don't believe you if you try to explain that the monster in their closet is really kind-hearted and adorable. In truth, we're not using the word "monster" in the normal sense when we do this. Instead, we're trying to change the word's meaning to refer more generally to creatures that aren't part of our normal, natural world. Being a monster implies being something unpleasant, repulsive, and very scary, which means you literally cannot like it. If you do, then it's not really a monster to you.

Supernatural and Philosophy: Metaphysics and Monsters ... for Idjits, First Edition.
Edited by Galen A. Foresman.
© 2013 John Wiley & Sons, Inc. Published 2013 by John Wiley & Sons, Inc.

Moving Backward to Move Forward

If our current conception of monster is out of whack, then maybe it will help to understand where the word comes from. Before English speakers adopted the word from the French, *monstre* and *mostre*, the word "monster" began its life much like any other word from the Romance languages, as a Latin word, *monstrum*, which translates as an evil and often unnatural sign or omen. The Latin root of *monstrum* is somewhat disputed, but essentially the word derives from either *monstro* or *moneo*. The former simply means to show, as it does in the word "demonstrate." The latter means to warn or advise, as it does in the Latin *monere* and later the English word "monitor." So basically, we've found that from meek and modest parentage, albeit disputed, we eventually get the abomination that is the word "monster." So maybe "monster" is really just misunderstood, and we should think of it as meaning something on display, hopefully to be learned from.

While this helps, it's not like a monster is an artifact in a museum. We know monsters aren't tamable in these ways, so they must be something more. And to understand what more that could be, Aristotle's (384—322 BCE) metaphysics can help. Metaphysics is the branch of philosophy that studies the nature of reality. Here, we'll focus on four areas Aristotle considered when determining what something really was, namely, essence, predicates, judgments, and potentials. Understanding and employing these concepts in our own concept of monster will help us avoid our currently tainted love of *Supernatural*.

Sam, I Am

Before getting into our own full-blown account of monsters, let's apply Aristotle's concepts to the monsters of *Supernatural*. After all, whatever our concept of monster turns out to be, it has to fit with the canon of our favorite show.

According to Aristotle, there are essential and accidental aspects of being. In the simplest terms, the essential aspects are the things that could not change about something, while the accidental aspects are things that could change. In the first season, Sam experienced significant heartache and death at the hands of a demon with yellow eyes, Azazel. After killing Sam's mother, Mary, Azazel kills Sam's girlfriend, Jessica. While both these events play important roles in making Sam the hunter he is today, Aristotle's distinction should lead us to wonder whether Sam's being a hunter is essential to his being or accidental. Is hunting an unchangeable part of Sam's being? Would Sam still be Sam if he were never a hunter? These are questions regarding Sam's essence. If it's possible that Sam could have lived a very different and domestic life, then hunting is an accidental aspect of Sam's being. Interestingly enough, Azazel reveals to Dean that it all started when their mother *accidently* got in the way, which seems to imply Sam's life could have been very different. Then again, Azazel is a demon and so he's naturally a liar, making it hard to know for sure.

Aristotle believed that a thing's being could be described in terms of ten categories, including substance, quantity, quality, and seven more. These categories are all things that can be *predicated of* or *said of* the being in question. In noting that Sam is a hunter, we were *categorizing* the substance of his being. Similarly, in saying, "Sam is 6 ft. 4 in. tall," we are categorizing his height according to quantity. As we did with his status as a hunter, we might ask if this height is essential or accidental to his being Sam. The answer is probably not. Sam could have been a little shorter or taller and still have been Sam.

In "Dead Man's Blood," John Winchester offers his Aristotelian expertise on some essentials to being a vampire:

> Most vampire lore is crap. A cross won't repel them. Sunlight won't kill them, and neither will a stake in the heart. But the blood lust … that part's true. They need fresh, human blood to survive. They were once people so you won't know it's a vampire until it's too late. (Season 1, Episode 20)

Here, John is describing the substance of being a vampire. It's an essential part of the substance of being a vampire that they look like humans, have eyes like humans, walk and talk like humans. In other ways, though, their essence is drastically different than humans. Most notably, they are ageless and they survive on blood.

Suppose we pointed at the Alpha-Vampire and asked, "What is this thing, this being?" and we were told, "That is thirteen." This would be a really weird response because the question was asking about the Alpha-Vampire's *substance*, but the response, "thirteen," is a *quantity*. In other words, we often ask questions of beings with specific categories in mind and, as this example illustrates, we expect answers that fit the categories we asked about. In our case, here, we asked a question of substance, not one of quantity, and so we expect an answer in the category of substance. As we will come to discuss later, this recognition paves the way for understanding the essence of demons and angels, particularly as they possess meat-suits and vessels. Moreover, it will also serve us well when we ask questions about what it is to be a monster.

Aristotle's third taxonomy of being is found in judgments of truth and falsity about a thing. These judgments can apply to questions of essence, accident, or any of the categories. They can also apply, as we'll see, to judgments of potentiality. In their first meeting, Dean and Castiel sort through judgments of being, so that Dean can understand what Castiel is. At first, Dean asks, "Who are you?" and Castiel replies, "Castiel." But this response doesn't fit the category that Dean had intended to ask about, so Dean corrects himself, "Yeah I figured that much. What are you?" Castiel replies, "An angel of the Lord."

In this bit of dialogue, truth and falsity play a central role. Once the categorical incongruence is cleared up, Dean wants to know the truth about Castiel's substance. Castiel claims to be an angel, but looks like a human. In fact, he's actually possessing a human vessel, so it's reasonable for Dean to feel like he's not getting the whole truth regarding Castiel's substance. We later learn that Castiel's true form is taller than the Chrysler Building. So, can a being's substance change? This brings us to the last important distinction from Aristotle, between actual and potential.

According to Aristotle, a being can be actual or potential. For example, a bird can be an actual bird or a potential bird. An actual bird is an animal with wings and feathers, whereas a potential bird is a fertilized egg, still needing to be hatched. Further, the egg is a bird only in the sense that it is a potential bird. Regarding actuality, the egg is just an egg. For Aristotle, the actual comes before the potential, because there must be some actual substance that has potential for some other specific actuality. Regarding Sam and Dean, we could say that they are potential demonic and angelic weapons during the fifth season, respectively, but their actuality of being during that time is human. Similarly, Castiel's actuality is angel, but we learn in the sixth season that he has the potential to be much more, maybe even God.

A Monster by Another Name

Having now armed ourselves with Aristotle's terminology and distinctions, it's time to return to our initial questions. Can we love monsters? If there's a monster in our kid's closet, could it be cute and nice? And ultimately, the most important question of all, can we love *Supernatural* because we love the monsters?

As we learned from our brief study of Latin at the beginning of this chapter, the word "monster" comes from a relatively innocuous lineage. To be sure, warnings and omens aren't exactly things we look forward to, but that's because we're concerned about what follows these signs, not the signs themselves. Using our taxonomy from Aristotle, we might say that warnings, omens, and signs are not essentially bad. In fact, many of us appreciate being given a warning, so that we can avoid the bad things that may be heading our way. But can the same be said for monsters? Or is it really essential to monsters that they be repulsive and always avoided?

Any question about the essential nature of monsters requires an answer that applies to all monsters. There are, of course, lots and lots of different monsters, but since we don't really care about anything else but our ability to freely love the monsters of *Supernatural*, we can exclude any others from our discussion. So the initial question for us to answer is how vampires, demons, wendigos, werewolves, and the various other monsters from *Supernatural* are all alike in their monstrousness?

As it turns out, Aristotle had a very robustly conceived taxonomy of substance that we could initially borrow from, but in the long run it would fail to tell us everything we want to know, since being a monster includes various genus/species categories. In other words, being a monster would be a very general category, like the category of things that move. In fact—because some monsters are what Aristotle called, "Ensouled Destructible Mobile Substances," which is the category that includes all living things, while other monsters are clearly, "Unensoulded Destructible Mobile Substances," which includes fire, earth, wind, water, and presumably, robots, golems, Sam without a soul, and even some demons who've sold their soul—the lowest we could really get on Aristotle's substance taxonomy is "Destructible Mobile Substances." This is a category so broad as to include anything that can be destroyed and that can also move itself about. So really, Aristotle's taxonomy of substances in the categories isn't all that helpful here.

There is a silver lining, though. We can now say that substance isn't what makes something a monster. But really, we could save ourselves the effort of working through all ten of Aristotle's categories of being, if we could just determine what monsters have in common that isn't also present in non-monsters. As an example, we might suggest an obvious commonality is that all monsters are beings that Sam and Dean hunt. But, unfortunately, this commonality will only take us so far, since it's not an essential commonality. If it were essential to being a monster that Sam and Dean hunt it, then there wouldn't have been monsters before Sam and Dean were hunters. Obviously, a better suggestion might be that monsters are all things that hunters hunt, but this would leave us with a similar problem, since we know monsters, like those in purgatory, have been around far longer than hunters.

What about the suggestion that all monsters are gross and repulsive? Are either of these essential to being a monster? No, being attractive doesn't automatically exclude something from the monster category. Obvious examples of this are all the monsters that use physical attraction to lure unsuspecting victims to their death. Vampires are notorious for this, as are arachnes, siren, succubae, incubi, and Amazons. Interestingly enough, the same really isn't true of demons. We're constantly reminded of the hideous true form of demons in *Supernatural*, which probably still haunts Sam long after his relationship with the demon Ruby.

Rather than start with a commonality among all types of monster, we might try looking at the differences between a human and a monster. More specifically, for those monsters that were originally human, we should find the important monster making-feature, gradually or abruptly appearing through that metamorphosis. For example, some humans become werewolves, and we've already agreed that werewolves are monsters. Thus, in Aristotle's terms, this means that even though the actuality for those humans is human, they are also potentially werewolves. In these people, we should be able to observe the monstrousness appearing. Granted, being a monster will only be one of the changes, but this is at least a start. We'll focus on the werewolf for now, but other possible examples of this transition occur with wendigo, Doc Benton, and rugarus.

In the episode "Heart," Sam and Dean meet Madison, a girl who doesn't know she's a werewolf. In Aristotle's terms, Madison spends most of her time as an actual human and potential monster. As a werewolf, she is an actual monster and potential human. One of the important changes that occur during this metamorphosis is that the person we've come to know as "Madison" seems to disappear. Her physical body changes dramatically, as does her personality and character. When the werewolf is present, Madison is gone. If we imagined this transformation with no physical changes, we'd have the body of Madison with the mind of a werewolf. Would this be a monster?

If this seems like a tricky question, simply ask yourself, "Given that this body is Madison's but it's being controlled by a werewolf, would I treat it like Madison or a werewolf?" This shows that being a monster has more to do with thoughts and actions than it does with appearance. Therefore, the essence of being a monster isn't in physical appearance. Further support for this claim comes from the Bender family, in the aptly named episode "The Benders." This family kidnaps people to hunt them for sport. Surely the thoughts and actions of these people are nothing short of monstrous. They may be human biologically, but they're definitely monsters in some other really essential way. This means that the examples of Madison and the Bender family considerably narrow our search for what it means to be a monster, since we can now be sure that physical appearance doesn't play an essential role in the concept.

Out with the Old

Of course, having just concluded the negligible, if non-existent, role that appearance plays in being a monster, we might still wonder why so many monsters are gross? Is it just coincidence, or is there some other factor we're not considering? At this point, I think it's worth noting that this judgment is *always* rendered by a human. Judging the appearance of a monster is a human behavior, and these judgments say more about us than the monsters they're intended to describe. In fact, it's really only on rare occasions that monsters judge the appearance or behavior of other monsters, and they almost never refer to one another as "monsters." So why do we do it?

The short answer is that most of us are "speciesist." We are prejudiced in elevating the human species over other species in terms of rights and values. We keep animals as pets, and many of us readily eat, wear, and sit on the flesh of other species. In many cases, monsters just treat humans the way we treat other animals. We fail to see the symmetry, though, since we place ourselves above all other species. Obviously, monsters aren't a species of being, but we are prejudiced and "speciesist" in placing humanity above animals and monsters. The ironically titled episode, "Jump the Shark," has some poignant and scathing dialogue regarding this bigoted relationship between humans and monsters:

SAM: Silver. No wonder none of the tests worked. You're not shapeshifters. You're ghouls.

GHOUL-KATE: You know, I find that term racist ...

SAM: I should have known. It was the fresh kills that threw me. Ghouls don't usually go after the living. See, you're just filthy scavengers, feeding off the dead— taking the form of the last corpse you choke down ...

GHOUL-KATE: Well, we are what we eat.
SAM: You're monsters.
GHOUL-ADAM: You know, you use that word a lot, Sam ... But I
                 don't think you know what it means ...

To Sam, the only relevant thing about ghouls is that they're monsters. The fact that under normal conditions ghouls don't kill people doesn't seem to matter at all. The ghouls are judged as not deserving the same rights and privileges humans have. Of course, you might try to defend Sam by saying that ghouls are dangerous and could decide to start killing and eating people, as these two did. But you could say that about all sorts of animals, including humans. So that wouldn't lead you to the conclusion that they should all be exterminated. Our ghoul friends also made this point with Sam:

GHOUL-ADAM: Our father was a monster? Why? Because of
                 what he ate? He never hurt anyone, Sam. Living,
                 anyway.

The simple truth in all of this is that we think so highly of humans that we're extremely offended when even a human corpse is eaten by a ghoul. In "The Benders" episode, Sam can't bring himself to kill Pa Bender, despite the fact that he's a murdering, cannibalistic hillbilly. Something about Pa's humanity prevented Sam from treating him like the monster that he was. Fortunately, Deputy Hudak saw through the façade and meted out justice accordingly.

The Monster at the End of This Chapter

It should be clear at this point that being a monster means having a particular relationship with humans. Monsters are monsters because they offend human sensibilities, and they do this by threatening to undermine the value we place on ourselves. Monsters don't value human lives over their own lives, and oddly enough, this bothers us. Notice how quickly some of the angels in *Supernatural* appear to be monsters because of how they treat humans. Compare that with how quickly the archangel Gabriel resumes his angelic status by defending humanity from his brother, Lucifer. If you had to eat dinner with either Crowley or Alastair, which would you be more comfortable with? Surely it's the one that transformed Hell from chains and torture to an endlessly long queue.

From the outset, we were concerned that monsters were the sorts of beings that we could not like, even if we tried. Our concern was that by liking them, they'd no longer be monsters, and then we'd be less interested in watching *Supernatural*. Well, I have bad news and good news. The bad news is that we've discovered that the very definition of being a monster prevents us from really liking them. The good news is that because we're prejudiced against monsters we love watching them hunted down and executed for daring to exist as our potential equals. As a result, we can all continue loving *Supernatural* and the monsters it contains, since it would clearly be hard to have one without the other.

Chapter 3

Hunters, Warriors, Monsters

Shannon B. Ford

Sam and Dean do a lot of killing. In fact, the Winchesters spend most of their time driving around the United States "killing as many evil sons of bitches" as they can. Normally, we think of killing as morally wrong, and under normal circumstances the amount of killing that Sam and Dean engage in is probably pathologically insane.[1] But, as we well know, the brothers don't live in an ordinary world. For starters, their mother was murdered by a mysterious yellow-eyed demon when they were children, and while that doesn't excuse everything they do, it was through this tragedy that they learned that horrific monsters do exist. Subsequently, they are brought up believing it's *right* to hunt them all down.

As hunters, Sam and Dean kill monsters because such creatures pose a threat to the lives of innocent people. But matters aren't that simple; Sam and Dean are confronted with a complex array of moral issues in killing. Although they frequently deliberate on the ethics of killing, the moral principles by which the Winchesters justify these actions are sometimes ambiguous. Things get really murky morally when they find it necessary to kill innocent humans. In fact, the ongoing conflict the Winchesters have with certain types of monsters in *Supernatural* might be better described as warfare rather than hunting. Often times, Sam and Dean display behavior and attitudes toward killing that calls to question whether "hunters" is the appropriate title for them at all.

Supernatural and Philosophy: Metaphysics and Monsters ... for Idjits, First Edition.
Edited by Galen A. Foresman.
© 2013 John Wiley & Sons, Inc. Published 2013 by John Wiley & Sons, Inc.

Eat it, *Twilight*!

Early on in *Supernatural* we learn that hunters are ordinary people who know of the hidden supernatural evil that exists in the world and choose to spend their lives fighting it. Hunting, as the name suggests, involves tracking down these creatures and figuring out a way to destroy them. There are three fundamentally important types of creature in *Supernatural*: monsters, spirits, and demons. Shapeshifters, for example, are a type of monster with the ability to mimic a person's physical appearance and access their thoughts. Spirits, on the other hand, are dangerous ghosts that have died violent deaths or are lashing out in revenge for other personal reasons. Finally, demons are creatures that escape Hell long enough to possess people and cause all varieties of havoc, sometimes purposeful and sometimes purely meaningless. Although there are many important differences among supernatural creatures, Sam and Dean use the generic term "monsters" as shorthand for categorizing all the creatures they hunt.[2]

For most hunters, the monstrous nature of these creatures makes them "evil" and justifies their being hunted. Since it is the nature of a monster to maim and kill innocent people, giving little or no thought to a person's humanity, hunters see it as their duty to kill such creatures to prevent the death of innocent victims. For the most part, hunters are really a lot more like exterminators than what we'd traditionally think of as hunters. Normally, we think of hunters as hunting for food, skins, or sport, but the hunters of *Supernatural* aren't ordinarily motivated to hunt monsters for any of these reasons. Even if a hunter enjoys their work, they probably wouldn't describe it as "sport." They certainly wouldn't eat the monster when they had killed it, and rarely do they take trophies from monsters to mount on their walls. Like most other exterminators, the hunters of *Supernatural* get rid of the monstrous pests and move on to the next job.

As hunters—or monster exterminators if you prefer—Sam and Dean are motivated to kill monsters in order to defend innocent people from being victims of those monsters. It follows, then, that from a moral standpoint Sam and Dean value personhood (or humanity) over the lives of the monsters they hunt. And we can relate to this—just think of all the pests we'd rather not have living in our homes, even if they aren't seriously threatening our lives. Most of us don't try to humanely remove cockroaches or fleas from our homes; we quickly resort to chemical warfare.

Sam and Dean begin hunting with a seemingly clear-cut distinction between humans and monsters, but as the series progresses black-and-white distinctions quickly turn grey. We find that some "monsters" exhibit many of the fundamentally good traits found in humanity, while conversely, many humans are undoubtedly monstrous. In other words, determining which creatures are pests for extermination is getting more difficult, since some people act horrifically toward other people. For example in "The Benders," Sam and Dean fight a family of humans who hunt and kill people for sport, which is pretty monstrous. This family is truly "hunting" in the traditional sense we discussed before, but they are hunting innocent people. In another clear example of a human crossing over the monstrous line, the episode "Time Is on My Side" has the brothers confronting Dr. Benton, a human who manages immortality by replacing his own decomposing organs with those of his victims. Given the opportunity to live in a similar fashion and avoid going to Hell, Dean decides that this type of immortality amounts to becoming a monster, which he finds unacceptable. On a related note, this is also Dean's main concern with going to Hell, since he fears it will turn him into one of the monsters he fears, loathes, and hunts.

On the flipside, there are some monsters that manage to reform themselves in such a way that they no longer threaten innocent people. Under normal circumstances, these would be the sort of monsters that Sam and Dean would exterminate. For example, in "Bloodlust," Sam is captured by a group of vampires. Their leader, Lenore, reveals to him that they have reformed and feed only on cattle. After being released unharmed, Sam eventually convinces his brother that the vampires should be left alone. In fact, Dean later admits to Sam that it would have been *wrong* to kill the vampires. And, of course, the idea that monsters can still retain their humanity is critically important for Sam, since he's concerned that he's changing into a monster himself. Hence, a central moral question for both Sam and Dean is whether a monster can maintain its humanity, and what is special about humanity that makes it worth protecting over the monsters they exterminate.

The Sanctity of Life and All That Crap

Of course, monsters aren't the only things Sam and Dean kill. They are also troubled by the frequent need to kill people who are not monsters, including innocent people possessed by malevolent demons. Sam and Dean know that killing people is wrong. In fact, the defense of people is often what justifies their killing of monsters. So what then are the primary moral issues involved in deciding to kill a human? And under what circumstances can Sam and Dean justify these killings?

All things being equal, most of us believe that killing a human is wrong. We recognize that to kill someone is to destroy something of considerable moral value, a human life. Some might argue that there is nothing about human life to morally distinguish it from other forms of life, but this view is typically rejected as implausible, since it makes a human life morally equivalent to bacteria and fungi. Ultimately, if we agree with the claim that it is wrong to kill another human, then we believe there is a basic right not to be killed by another person. If a monster is sufficiently like a human, then the monster may have the same right. Importantly, whether we're dealing with a human or a monster, this right is not absolute. There are some situations in which killing a person is justified provided we have the right reasons.

The strongest justifications for killing another person are the defense of your life or the lives of others.[3] In a case of self-defense, one is morally justified in killing an attacker when it is necessary to prevent one's own death at the hands of the attacker. For example, in "Dream a Little Dream of Me," Sam is attacked by Jeremy, who has been killing people Freddy Krueger-style in their dreams. When Jeremy attempts to kill Sam with a baseball bat, Sam manages to kill Jeremy first in self-defense. Had Jeremy not been killed, then Sam would have probably died from the attack. Since Jeremy is attempting to kill Sam, it is permissible for Sam to kill Jeremy in defense of his own life.

Similarly, we are justified in killing someone to defend the life of another person. Consider "Simon Said," in which Andy Weems kills his twin brother, Ansem, who is about to kill Dean. Ansem has the supernatural ability to control people's actions and is in the process of making Dean shoot himself. Andy justifiably intervenes to save Dean by shooting Ansem first.

Three features of the attacks make the killings permissible. First, the attacker is an immediate deadly threat. Jeremy and Ansem's attacks would have been deadly without immediate intervention. Second, the attacks are not justified. Jeremy's attack is motivated by his desire to continue his "dreaming," which has proved harmful to others. Sam is attacked unjustly after attempting to reason with Jeremy about his harmful actions. In the other case, Ansem was about to kill Andy's ex-girlfriend, Tracey, by making her jump off a bridge, so Ansem was stopped with a bullet. Third, the attacker in both cases was morally culpable.[4] Jeremy and Ansem were both fully responsible for threatening the life of another person, such that their own deaths were essentially brought on by their own choices.

Ultimately, it's clear that human life is important for Sam and Dean, and most of what they do is aimed at saving human life. If they do need to kill a person, then it is often justified in the defense of another human life. While Sam and Dean are less concerned with the monsters they kill, the more human a monster is, the more likely Sam and Dean are to leave it alone. The caveat here is, of course, when that monster poses a potential risk for humans in the future.

Nobody Kill Any Virgins!

Often, Sam and Dean find themselves needing to decide whether killing a human is worth the benefits that may result. Notably, this is not an issue they typically have with monsters. With monsters, the default is almost always kill first and live with the consequences. However, with humans, it's a very different picture. Sam and Dean have rules about when *not* to kill someone. Even if killing a person would serve a greater purpose, the Winchesters won't kill a person who is a bystander or who is not a deadly threat.

For example, in the episode "Jus in Bello," Sam and Dean are trapped in a police station when a horde of demons take control of the local population. The demon, Ruby, proposes a spell to kill all of the demons surrounding the station, but Dean refuses because it involves sacrificing a virgin. Despite the fact that the spell would have saved everyone in the station and most of the innocent towns-people outside, Dean doesn't think they are justified in killing the virgin, Nancy. Even when Nancy consents to being sacrificed in order save her possessed friends, Dean declares with his usual tact, "I'm not going to let the demon kill some sweet innocent girl that hasn't even been laid yet."

Furthermore, the brothers won't kill someone who isn't a threat, even if they previously had been. In "The Benders," Sam overpowers Lee and Jared Bender before shooting Pa Bender, rendering him harmless but alive. Rather than finish the job, Sam gives the rifle to the sheriff, Kathleen, so she can take the Benders into her custody. Instead, Kathleen shoots Pa Bender dead to avenge her murdered brother. Although Sam and Dean often have opportunities to kill people in this way, it's an unjust and immoral line they don't cross.

There's an Innocent Girl Trapped Somewhere in There?

A tricky moral problem arises for Sam and Dean concerning the killing of innocent victims possessed by demons. A possessed person has no ability to control her actions; she is reduced to being a puppet manipulated by the demon, what demons cruelly refer to as a "meatsuit."

We are first introduced to an innocent person possessed by a demon in the form of Meg Masters, a young girl Sam meets while hitchhiking in "Scarecrow." Meg was possessed attending college and, while possessed, Meg is sometimes conscious of the demon's actions, even though she is helpless to stop them. People like Meg are not only innocent of the wrongs committed by the demon possessing them, but they are also very much the kind of innocent people Sam and Dean feel obligated to protect.

Unfortunately, Sam and Dean still do sometimes knowingly kill these innocent people who happen to be possessed. One reason for this is that a person whose body is being possessed by a demon might already be dead; but it's hard to know for sure. Furthermore, lethal force harms only the human meatsuit, not the demon possessing it. In fact, this is how Sam and Dean inadvertently kill the human Meg when they cause her to be defenestrated from the seventh floor of a warehouse in the episode "Shadow." When Sam and Dean later exorcise the demon possessing her in "Devil's Trap," the human Meg dies from the injuries she sustained in the fall.

Sam and Dean learn a valuable lesson from their experience with Meg, and so they are fully aware that they are killing innocent people in addition to the demons that possess them. To that end, Sam and Dean generally stick to their belief that killing an innocent person possessed by a demon is *only* allowable when they have no other realistic alternative. In other words, they should really try not to kill possessed people, but they may do so when killing them is self-defense or in the defense of others. The right to defend a life comes from the fact that a victim is in danger of losing their life. It doesn't have anything to do with whether the attacker is in control of their actions.[5] As long as Sam and Dean are trying to defend an innocent life, they may kill a possessed person. If they didn't, then the possessed meatsuit would unjustly violate another innocent person's right to live.

Still, Sam and Dean often take significant risks to rescue the innocent person who is possessed. In fact, this concern is one of the driving motivations for Sam to harness the powers given to him by the demon Azazel, which gives him the ability to easily exorcise demons. Ultimately, when it is necessary to kill a possessed person, Sam and Dean believe the killing should always be carried out reluctantly followed by regret (but absolutely no tears). Sam and Dean regularly express their moral concern for the fate of the innocent people possessed by demons, especially those whom it is necessary to kill. Furthermore, both brothers are fearful of becoming hardened by the killing. They do not wish it to become something they find easy to do. This problem is illustrated by the moral deterioration we observe in a fellow hunter, Gordon, who has learned to enjoy killing. Dean explicitly rejects this "moral flexibility" when Gordon tries to convince him it's okay. In a sense, Gordon has moved on from the job of exterminating evil monsters to the enjoyable sport of hunting.

We're Not Just Hunting Anymore: We're at War!

In "What's Up, Tiger Mommy?" Sam kills a demon after performing a reverse exorcism to pull a demon back into the body of an innocent person, preventing it from passing on crucial information to other demons. By their own ethical standards, Sam and Dean would normally consider this type of killing cold-blooded murder. How can it possibly be morally justified?

In Season 8, the Winchesters discover there might be a spell to banish all demons from the world and keep them out forever. This might justify a temporary change in their ethics of killing. Rather than being hunters, we might argue Sam and Dean are combatants in a war against demons. In the episode "Malleus Maleficarum," Sam even points out that their ongoing battle against demons is more like fighting a war than simply hunting, and the demon Ruby chastises Sam and Dean at the end of "Jus in Bello" because they don't seem to know how to fight a war.

As hunters, Sam and Dean follow typical rules of morality when dealing with people, but if they're warriors, those rules might change significantly. Warriors are bound by "Just War Theory," which gives combatants special permissions for killing enemy combatants.[6] The just war tradition attempts to explain the "rightness" or "wrongness" of the decision to go to war (*jus ad bellum*) and the "rightness" and "wrongness" of the way in which a war is conducted (*jus in bello*).[7] Importantly, just war theory permits combatants in a war to do certain types of harms that are not allowed in a non-war context.[8] For example, combatants fighting a war can attack and kill enemy combatants without warning, as they might in a missile strike or ambush. They are also permitted to do serious collateral harm, including killing and maiming non-combatants. Bombing a city, after all, includes bombing those people who just happen to be living there. But this is only allowed provided that the military objective is important enough to justify the foreseeable deaths of non-combatants.

At this point in the series, Sam and Dean are making a moral distinction between the two different roles of "hunter" and "warrior." In their role as warriors, they would be permitted to commit killings that would otherwise be morally unjustifiable.[9]

I Might Be a Freak, But That's Not the Same as Dangerous

Under normal circumstances, Sam and Dean are monster exterminators. When it comes to killing, they rarely hesitate to destroy a monster. In fact, they're often more willing to be merciful with evil, dangerous people than they would otherwise be with a monster. What's more, the Winchesters generally give no justification for this bias. And when they're confronted with this contradiction in their moral thinking, they normally awkwardly muddle through it. Nevertheless, this bias returns season after season in one episode or another.

Perhaps the most salient example occurs in "The Girl Next Door." A kitsune child named Amy befriends Sam, and even kills her own mother to save Sam's life. As an adult, Amy doesn't kill people until its very own child becomes sick and needs fresh pituitary glands to survive. In desperation, Amy kills several people to save the life of her child.

After tracking Amy down and realizing that it's his old friend from childhood, Sam sees no reason to kill her because her son is now healthy, and she no longer has a reason to kill. What good would it do when she is no longer a threat? It isn't as though she *wants* to kill anyone.

Sam explains the situation to Dean who promises to leave Amy alone. But then Dean tracks Amy down anyway and kills her. Before killing Amy, Dean justifies himself to her by saying, "But people ... they are who they are. No matter how hard you try, you are what you are. You will kill again ... Trust me, I'm an expert."

Unfortunately, it's a little difficult to know what Dean thinks he's an expert on here. If he thinks he's an expert on people, then he should recognize that he's not dealing with a human. After all, he kills her like he would any other monster. So, what he's saying doesn't really make sense, and it certainly doesn't make sense as a justification for killing Amy. No, to make sense of this, Dean would have to be suggesting he's an expert on monsters, like an exterminator's an expert on the bugs and rodents she exterminates. But if that's the case, how does Dean fail to see that he's far more "monstrous" than Amy? Dean has killed more innocent people than Amy, and he knows that he killed at least some of them for the wrong reasons. The difficulty here is that no matter how much we want to justify Dean's actions, he is what he is, and when he occasionally indulges in the type of "moral flexibility" that allows him to kill with impunity, Dean is worse than many of the monsters he hunts.

Notes

1. Dean, in particular, is arrested on a number of occasions by the FBI as a suspected serial killer.
2. As the series progresses, Sam and Dean come across other types of creatures in the "Supernatural" universe, such as "pagan gods," "angels," "reapers" and the Horsemen of the Apocalypse (including Death himself). But the primary focus is on the three main groups. In the more recent seasons we also discover the leviathans, a fourth type of evil creature with characteristics of both demons and monsters, which presents a new suite of problems for the brothers.
3. For discussion of the philosophy of killing in self-defense and defense of others, see: Jonathan Quong, "Liability to Defensive Harm," *Philosophy & Public Affairs* 40, no. 1 (2012): 45–77. Jonathan Quong, "Killing in Self-Defense," *Ethics* 119, no. 3 (2009): 507–537; Jeff McMahan, "The Basis of Moral Liability to Defensive Killing," *Philosophical Issues* 15, no. 1 (2005): 386–405; Seumas Miller, "Killing in Self-Defense," *Public Affairs Quarterly* 7, no. 4 (1993): 325–339; Suzanne Uniacke, *Permissible Killing: The Self-Defence Justification of Homicide* (Cambridge: Cambridge University Press, 1994); Fiona Leverick, *Killing in*

Self-Defence (Oxford: Oxford University Press, 2006); Judith J. Thomson, "Self-Defense," *Philosophy & Public Affairs* 20, no. 4 (1991): 283–310.

4. An agent is fully culpable for a threat of harm when the following conditions are met: (1) the agent acts in a way that results in a threat of impermissible harm to an innocent person (or persons); (2) the agent intends or foresees this harm, or else is acting recklessly or neg-ligently; and (3) there are no relevant excusing conditions (e.g., blame-less ignorance, duress, or diminished responsibility). Quong, "Liability to Defensive Harm," 50.

5. Uniacke, *Permissible Killing: The Self-Defence Justification of Homicide*, 185.

6. For a discussion on just war theory and the ethics of killing in war, see: Michael Walzer, *Just and Unjust Wars: A Moral Argument with Historical Illustrations*, 4th edn (New York: Basic Books, 2006); Jeff McMahan, *Killing in War* (Oxford: Oxford University Press, 2009); David Rodin, *War and Self-Defense* (New York: Oxford University Press, 2003); Brian Orend, *The Morality of War* (Ontario: Broadview Press, 2006); Fritz Allhoff, Nicholas G. Evans, and Adam Henschke, *Routledge Handbook of Ethics and War: Just War Theory in the 21st Century* (London: Taylor & Francis, 2013).

7. I won't describe the tenets of the just war tradition here but for an excellent (and short) overview, read: David Whetham, "The Just War Tradition: A Pragmatic Compromise," in *Ethics, Law and Military Operations*, ed. David Whetham (Basingstoke: Palgrave Macmillan, 2011), 65–89.

8. S. Brandt Ford, "Jus Ad Vim and the Just Use of Lethal Force-Short-Of-War," in *Routledge Handbook of Ethics and War: Just War Theory in the 21st Century*, ed. Fritz Allhoff, Nicholas G. Evans, and Adam Henschke (Taylor & Francis, 2013), ch. 6.

9. For more on exceptionalism, see: Andrew Fiala, "A Critique of Exceptions: Torture, Terrorism, and the Lesser Evil Argument," *International Journal of Applied Philosophy* 20, no. 1 (2005): 127–142; Fritz Allhoff, *Terrorism, Ticking Time-Bombs, and Torture: A Philosophical Analysis* (Chicago: University of Chicago Press, 2012), esp. Chapter 3, 35–56; Jonathan H. Marks, "What Counts in Counterterrorism," *Columbia Human Rights Law Review* 37, no. 3 (2005): 559–626.

Chapter 4

Team Free Will
Something Worth Fighting For

*Devon Fitzgerald Ralston and
Carey F. Applegate*

Supernatural begins with a flashback. Dean Winchester and his mother, Mary, are saying goodnight to his brother, Sam. His father, John, walks in and rounds out the scene of the family of four. A few hours later, Mary hears Sam crying and goes to the nursery where she sees a man standing over the crib. Assuming it's John, Mary walks away, but notices the television downstairs and sees John sleeping in front of it. Rushing back to protect her son, she is pinned to the ceiling and killed in a horrific fire. Ultimately, Dean, Sam, and John escape the fire, but they can't seem to escape its impact on their lives. This leads us to wonder if Sam and Dean really had a choice in becoming hunters. If not, are they now ethically bound to these roles as saviors? Could they refuse this life, hang it up, walk away?

Throughout *Supernatural*, we watch the Winchesters resist, embrace, and redefine their roles in the family business, "saving people, hunting things." These tensions echo a topic that philosophers have explored for thousands of years—free will. Free will is typically understood as the ability of individuals to choose courses of action for their lives based on their ability to reason freely. Free will is often set against determinism, the theory that every event is entirely explainable in terms of prior events, including prior choices.

Supernatural and Philosophy: Metaphysics and Monsters ... for Idjits, First Edition.
Edited by Galen A. Foresman.

As we'll see, though, the debate over free will and determinism is more complicated than it first appears.

The Family Business

Much of *Supernatural* is devoted to exploring the Winchesters' potential futures. Part of this exploration includes looking into how their choices are impacted by external forces, including events from their past. For example, Sam never wanted the life of a hunter, but whether he likes it or not, it seems that he and Dean are destined to carry on this family tradition. Prior to their birth, plans were made to ensure their existence. In "My Bloody Valentine," we learn Heaven ordered a cupid to couple their parents, John and Mary. Even when Mary pulls away from hunting to create a normal life with John, events align to bring her back into the hunting community. All this suggests that, regardless of their choices, powerful external forces manipulate and shape the Winchesters' lives, illustrating the philosophical concept of determinism, according to which the past, present, and future form an unalterable chain of events.

Sam and Dean are often pressed to believe that their fates have been predetermined. Zachariah, for example, reveals how moments in their family history make the events of Sam and Dean's lives inevitable. One such example is Azazel's bargain with Mary over John's life in "The Song Remains the Same." This bargain sets the family on a seemingly inescapable path, first by allowing Azazel to enter Sam's nursery without interference and then costing Mary her own life when she very naturally tries to protect him. This loss pushes John, never a hunter before, to fixate on killing Azazel along with as many evil things as he possibly can. Consequently, John raises Sam and Dean in the life Mary tried so hard to escape, a life she never wanted for any of them. According to Zachariah, this chain of events ultimately led to Sam and Dean being the chosen vessels for the apocalyptic showdown between the archangel Michael and his brother, Lucifer.

Given Zachariah's synopsis, the Winchesters' lives appear predetermined; their roles as hunters and vessels were decided before they existed. Indeed, angels of all stripes repeatedly try to convince Sam and Dean of the fruitless nature of fighting their destiny. The brothers are sent to the past, future, and alternate realities, so that they may understand that they are subject to a particular prearranged fate. Fortunately, the brothers' stubborn nature serves them well, as they refuse to accept that their lives have been predetermined. During a conversation with the archangel Michael in "The Song Remains the Same," Dean resists playing a role in the Apocalypse:

MICHAEL: And you think you know better than my Father? One unimportant little man? What makes you think you get to choose?

DEAN: Because I gotta believe that I can choose what I do with my unimportant little life.

MICHAEL: You're wrong. You know how I know? Think of a million random acts of chance that let John and Mary be born, to meet, to fall in love, to have the two of you. Think of the million random choices that you make and yet how each and every one of them brings you closer to your destiny. Do you know why that is? Because it's not random. It's not chance. It's a plan that is playing itself out perfectly. Free will is an illusion, Dean. That's why you are going to say yes.

Rarely does Dean refuse to play his part as a Winchester or hunter. In fact, Dean goes to great lengths to maintain those parts of his identity. But here Dean rejects Michael's assertion that "free will is an illusion" and defies his purported destiny. In so doing, Dean proudly joins the ranks of "Team Free Will." A group proudly composed of "one ex-blood junkie, one dropout with 6 bucks to his name, and Mr. Comatose ..."

Free Will and Bad Faith

According to the existentialist philosopher Jean-Paul Sartre (1905–1980), each person is in a constant state of shaping himself and his place in the world through free will. Sartre believed we could break free of our pasts, from society's expectations, and from the conditioning of our behavior, all by affirming ourselves through new choices and actions. In fact, Sartre argues that we have no pre-given essence, and so we make ourselves who we are through our free choices and actions. We are completely free and responsible for the choices we make, but as a result we experience anguish. Accepting Sartre's philosophy means accepting that for better or worse the Winchesters can only hold themselves accountable for their lives.

Free will requires an ability to do otherwise.[1] For example, Mary could have let John die rather than making a deal with Azazel, which means Mary was acting freely when she made the deal with Azazel. Similarly, following Mary's death, John could have raised his sons differently, not as hunters. As a result of being able to choose other than they did, the free choices of the Winchesters directly express how much they value things like devotion to family, saving lives, and atoning for guilt.

Because of the heavy burden of responsibility, we don't always appreciate our ability to make free choices. Instead we are tempted to act in what Sartre calls "bad faith," lying to ourselves by denying our freedom and believing that luck, fate, or God's plan determine our choices and absolve us of responsibility. Dean is admirable in his ability to resist bad faith and act as captain for Team Free Will. Despite the pressure, he asserts that he has the choice to refuse as Michael's vessel. He is not in denial, not in bad faith, but instead chooses his own sense of right and wrong.

The same can't always be said for Sam. His rebellion and attempted self-expression are in bad faith to the extent that they are forged in lies Sam tells himself about his choices. Sam is only able to be truly free when he finally accepts personal responsibility and stops blaming family expectations for his choices.

Family Matters in Moral Responsibility

Supernatural privileges values of family and loyalty above all else. John is consumed with grief and out for vengeance, so Dean takes responsibility for Sam. Dean constantly reminds Sam that he has this responsibility, and by the second season it is evident that the brothers take responsibility for one another, further reinforcing their commitment to family and the loyalty they have to one another. Only when one of them veers from this morality are drastic choices made, often resulting in irreparable consequences to their relationship. Sam does this when he drinks demon blood, and Dean does likewise when he keeps secret his memories of Hell.

At times in *Supernatural*, this responsibility to family is portrayed as potentially dangerous. As Dean says to Sam, "Killing that guy, killing Meg, I didn't hesitate. I didn't even flinch. For you or Dad, the things I'm willing to do or kill, it scares me sometimes." The archangel Gabriel, disguised as a trickster, echoes this sentiment in "Mystery Spot" during a conversation with Sam about Dean's impending trip to Hell:

> This obsession to save Dean, the way you two keep sacrificing yourselves for each other, nothing good comes out of it, just blood and pain. Dean's your weakness, and the bad guys know it, too. It's gonna be the death of you, Sam. Sometimes you just gotta let people go.

Of course, Sam doesn't heed Gabriel's advice. Doing so would mean denying his primary responsibility to Dean, who, ironically, is going to Hell as a direct result of his devotion to Sam. In "Point of No Return," Zachariah warns Sam and Dean's half-brother, Adam, about the depths of devotion they have for one another, "Didn't we tell you about them? So you know you can't trust them, right? You know Sam and Dean Winchester are psychotically, irrationally, erotically codependent on each other, right?"

From his introduction, Adam is excluded from what he calls "this whole dewy-eyed bromance thing." Because he was raised outside of the hunting life, his story serves as a counter-narrative, a possibility of what Sam and Dean's lives might have been. It also helps clarify how the Winchesters define their family. Sam and Dean accept Adam as a brother, sharing similar but distinct experiences with their father. But unfortunately for Adam, as we see in "Appointment in Samarra," a short-lived history and blood bond are not enough for Dean to pick him over Sam when Dean's given the chance to save one of them from Hell. Despite the occasionally contentious nature of their relationship, Sam is the brother to whom Dean feels the most loyalty and moral responsibility. Dean's choice and subsequent lack of emotion clearly display his view of Adam. They may be related, but they aren't family.

Sam and Dean do expand their familial circle beyond blood to Castiel and Bobby, however. With that expansion, all the actions and responsibilities that go with family and loyalty are expanded as well. For example, Dean tries to defuse an atomic Castiel-God after absorbing Purgatory's souls. In "The Man Who Knew Too Much," Dean says, "I know that there's a lot of bad water under the bridge, but we were family once. I'd have died for you. I almost did a few times." But even after the break-up of Team Free Will and the devastating emotional impact of Castiel-God's response, "You're not my family, Dean. I have no family," Dean still loves him like a brother, mournfully retrieving and folding Castiel's trench coat after Cas, bloated with leviathan, disappears into a lake.

As dangers come as a result of Sam and Dean's responsibility to one another, so too Dean's relationship with Cas comes with dangers of its own. Dean's loyalty to Castiel pushes Dean to cross lines he wouldn't otherwise cross. In "On the Head of a Pin," Dean tortures the demon Alastair at Cas's request, using techniques he learned from Alastair while in Hell. This pushes Dean into an intensely dark place, forcing him to recall experiences in the Pit, a considerable sacrifice to his own mental well-being. And he endures it all because Cas asked him to. As he was with his dad and Sam, Dean is willing to do scary things for those he considers family. In so doing, he proves his loyalty to Cas, strengthening their relationship but changing some of what he's willing to do, morally speaking.

Similarly, Bobby's relationship with Sam and Dean impacts their moral views and responsibilities. Although Bobby is first introduced simply as a family friend and fellow hunter, it turns out that he has a long history with the boys, having known them when they were young, and sometimes filling the paternal role when their father was away hunting. As Bobby is dying in "Death's Door," he's no longer just a temporary substitute for their father. He says, "As fate would have it, I adopted two boys. And they grew up great. They grew up heroes." Bobby is one of the few people who force Sam and Dean to set aside their responsibilities as hunters to embrace their family obligations. Afraid to lose this perspective, Sam and Dean can't bring themselves to burn Bobby's flask and free his ghost. Since they do this knowing Bobby is devolving into a vengeful spirit, this is yet another example of the dangerous degree of loyalty Sam and Dean have for those they regard as family.

Whether one views family loyalty as a strength or weakness, it is the most significant moral guidepost in Sam and Dean's lives. Above everything else they value, it exercises the greatest influence on their will. Given this influence, we should wonder how free this will really is.

How Free Can a Will Be and Still Be Free?

According to the philosopher David Hume (1711–1776), if our choices are unexplainable, if there isn't any cause for them, or reason for us to make them, then they don't really count as our choices, much less free choices. Our choices must come from our characters, what we value, and what we care about. Otherwise, they're not really our choices.

Hume's point is that our choices must have causes, but this doesn't mean they're determined. Family values and loyalty greatly impact Sam and Dean's choices, but these choices are still made freely. But is a person free when they choose to do something that they do not want to do? For example, does Dean freely allow Sam to sacrifice is soul to Hell by becoming Lucifer's vessel in an elaborate attempt to avoid the Apocalypse?

A two-stage model of free will allows for subtler distinctions in free will, which may help in the case of Sam and Dean.[2] In this model, the first stage of free will involves an individual mentally exploring a variety of possibilities, while the second stage involves that same individual choosing one among those options. This two-stage model helps account for more complicated issues regarding free will. For example, a woman with severe clinical depression may desire a more positive attitude, but be unable to affect change in her attitude, because of the physical and chemical nature of the disease. Despite the fact that she isn't physically restrained, she still doesn't really have free will. The disease is limiting the options from which she might legitimately choose. Similarly, a man struggling with alcoholism might desire to break free of his addiction. He might *want* to get sober, but find that he's physically unable to accomplish that goal. In other cases, a person may even be in a mental space where "wanting to become sober" isn't even a thought that crosses their mind, making its attainment by choice impossible.

These examples demonstrate that freedom of the will is bound, in part, to a complex understanding of human psychology. Does Dean freely allow Sam to sacrifice his life? Allowing this sacrifice runs contrary to a central value in Dean's life—caring for his brother—which indicates this is not a freely made choice. Dean makes a point of expressing his displeasure with this plan, but he also concedes to it in a conversation with Death during "Two Minutes to Midnight." Bobby puts the issue in stark relief, "So I got to ask, Dean. What exactly are you afraid of? Losing? Or losing your brother?"

In *Supernatural* the choices people make are impacted by their soul. In effect, the soul acts like a moral filter or compass guiding an individual's choices. While the soul does not force a particular option on an individual, in terms of the two-stage model of free will, it does limit which options are available. A being that lacks a soul seems to lack moral limits. For example, when Sam returns from Hell without his soul, he crosses ethical lines in ways that would have been previously unthinkable for him. In fact, Sam doesn't even register a hint of apprehension at allowing Dean to be turned into a vampire, making Dean fair game to hunters. But is this degree of freedom really freedom?

In "Family Matters," the Alpha-Vampire notes, "Amazing how that pesky little soul gets in the way, but not for you. You will be the perfect animal." Like the demons he fights, Soulless Sam shrugs off both the sense of responsibility and the problem of anguish that comes with caring that his choices may have negative consequences

for those around him. Soulless Sam has more options, but this actually makes him less free and responsible. As Hume reminds us,
"where [actions] proceed not from some cause in the character and
disposition of the person who performed them, they can neither
redound to his honor, if good; nor infamy, if evil."

Moral Responsibility and Anguish

The Winchesters are sometimes tortured by an acute awareness
that they could have chosen differently, and had they done so, the
lives of many other people would have been different. We see one
example of this in "What Is and What Should Never Be." Under the
influence of a djinn, Dean experiences a life where his mother
didn't die, and he and Sam didn't become hunters. Dean quickly
recognizes the ramifications of these changes, while people like
Mary and Jess live, people who Sam, Dean, and John previously
saved have now died. The brothers barely speak to one another. In
the climax of the episode, Dean stabs himself to get free of the
djinn's illusion while Sam and Mary from the illusion beg him to
stay. Dean's anguish in this moment is obvious, because it forces
him to weigh the lives of those he cares about with the lives of
those he's saved. When he and Sam discuss this later, Sam tries to
console Dean over the sacrifices they've made in their lives, "...
people are alive because of you. It's worth it, Dean. It is. It's not fair,
and y'know it hurts like Hell, but it's worth it." While Dean agrees,
"saving people, hunting things" is important, we see him, for the
first time since John's death, question whether the burden of doing
so is too much.

We see more fully the impact of anguish on Sam and Dean in the
eighth season. Sam understands the dangers of wanting normalcy
in his life, recognizing that everyone close to him becomes a liability
and another potential point of anguish down the road. Everything
Sam has gone through forces him to question his previous choices
and his previously constructed morality. In essence, anguish has Sam
questioning who he is and whether he's doing something worth-
while. Because of this anguish, once Sam is truly alone—losing

Dean to Purgatory, losing the central pillar to his identity in family and loyalty, losing so much of his identity in these things—he quits hunting.

In the midst of Sam losing his religion, Dean has been fighting for survival in Purgatory. Upon his return, he finds Sam has quit hunting, endangering the lives of the people he sacrificed himself to protect. The anguish that has driven Dean in Purgatory devolves into anger, resentment, and even righteous indignation. Infuriated, Dean repeatedly chastises Sam for this choice until Sam finally retorts that "free will is only for [Dean]." Sam's ability to move beyond hunting surprises Dean. Knowing that Sam could simply walk away from hunting to pursue a normal life shows Dean that they no longer share the same sense of moral responsibility.

Go Team!

While early seasons of *Supernatural* may convince the audience that Sam and Dean's futures have been predetermined by the machinations of angels, alternative-world episodes suggest that the brothers' lives are shaped by the choices they make with free will. For good or for ill, Sam and Dean are responsible for their actions, which is better than you'd expect from an ex-blood junkie and a high school dropout with six dollars in his pocket.

Notes

1. Thomas Hobbes, *Leviathan* (London: Penguin Books, 1968).
2. William James first proposed this two-stage model in a talk entitled "The Dilemma of Determinism," and numerous other philosophers have expanded upon it over the years.

Chapter 5

What the Hell Is Going On?

Galen A. Foresman

Don't get me wrong, I think I can understand why a person might sell their soul to a crossroads demon. There's something they really, really want, and there's simply no other way to get it, or just no other way to get it quickly. So you want to be the best blues musician of all time but you only just started learning the guitar, well then the crossroads demon may be your only way. But seriously, you do know what that deal gets you, right?

In case you've forgotten, and most people do, after ten years of living with whatever dream-come-true wish you made, your soul becomes the personal property of whatever demon you signed it over to in the original contract. Sometimes, the crossroads demon you're working with is a mere sales associate, getting a small commission for their efforts with you, while some big fat-cat demon is actually the one who ends up possessing your soul when everything is said and done. The devil, as they say, is in the details.

Now suppose your ten years have come due, and the demon's hell-hound is tearing down your door—was it worth it? Was a future of eternal suffering worth whatever it was that you got from the demon? Mary makes a deal with a demon for John's life; John makes a deal with a demon to save Dean's life; Dean makes a deal with a demon to save Sam's life; and eventually, Sam just ends up

Supernatural and Philosophy: Metaphysics and Monsters ... for Idjits, First Edition.
Edited by Galen A. Foresman.
© 2013 John Wiley & Sons, Inc. Published 2013 by John Wiley & Sons, Inc.

in the Cage with Lucifer anyway. Granted, these are deals to save the lives of other people, but are they really worth it?

No doubt, avoiding the Apocalypse was a good thing, and as a result of these deals, the Apocalypse was averted. But there may not have been an Apocalypse in the first place had Mary, John, and Dean not made their deals in the first place. After all, Dean's time in Hell resulted in the breaking of the first seal. But even if the Apocalypse had occurred anyway, then everyone who died in the Apocalypse would have gone to Heaven, not Hell. Furthermore, Mary, John, Dean, and Sam would never have had to spend any time in Hell either. It wasn't as though the deals struck by Mary, John, or Dean were deals that prevented someone from going to Hell. They merely brought people back to life, here on Earth.

At the end of the day, these deals with crossroads demons certainly make *Supernatural* exciting. They also help explain why there are so many demons in Hell. The answer is that these deals are really just clever pyramid schemes. Like all pyramid schemes, it's a really attractive offer until you realize that being on the bottom of the pyramid is really terrible, and only a few people make it to the top. Furthermore, making it to the top requires you to get new people to step all over on your way up. And even once you've reached the top, you're still just at the top of Hell, which isn't all that great.

Given all of this, I'm baffled by how regularly these deals occur. Even assuming your time in Hell wasn't the worst possible suffering imaginable for a virtually infinite amount of time, absolutely nothing seems valuable enough to warrant a voluntary trip there. Those souls that are there wish they weren't, and those making choices that will put them there, clearly do not understand the choices they're making.

Given all this, I think it's only natural to wonder what's the point of Hell in *Supernatural*?

The Road to Hell

Despite the popularity of phrases like, "Hell yeah!" and "Raise Hell!" the going theory for Hell is that it's not really a place for having a good time. Hell is a place souls go to be punished for the sins they committed on Earth. In "Born Under a Bad Sign" the demon Meg points out quite resentfully that Hell is bad even for the demons that live there:

> You know when people want to describe the worst possible thing? They say it's like Hell. You know there's a reason for that. Hell is like, um, well, it's like Hell. Even for demons. It's a prison, made of bone and flesh and blood and fear; and you sent me back there.

According to Christian theology, after being properly judged, bad souls are damned to Hell for eternity. *Supernatural* differs in that some of the souls in Hell weren't even judged, they just made very bad deals. But regardless of whether you think the mythos of *Supernatural* is even correct on this point, the fact that we recognize these are very bad deals should tell us something about the choices that land us in Hell, particularly if it's meant as a punishment.

I Saw *Hellraiser*, I Get the Gist

Normally, punishments are perceived as bad by the people who receive them. We don't like punishments, and we do what we can to avoid them. Our attitudes and emotions toward receiving punishment can range, but very rarely are they positive. Conversely, our attitudes and emotions toward punishing someone for having wronged us can often be positive. In fact, we may respond positively to punishing someone who has done something wrong, even if the wrong was not done to us personally. In "Family Remains," Dean confesses to feeling very guilty for what he did in Hell:

> I enjoyed it, Sam. They took me off the rack and I tortured souls and I liked it. All those years; all that pain. Finally getting to deal some out yourself. I didn't care who they put in front of me, because that pain I felt, it just slipped away. No matter how many people I save, I can't change that. I can't fill this hole. Not ever.

Whether we're doling out or receiving punishment, we have strong feelings about it, and these feelings tell us quite a bit about what punishment really is. For example, if you were told that a new prison had opened that pampered inmates with massages and personal chefs, your emotional reaction would probably indicate that you think this treatment is inappropriate, that it's not the way punishment *should* be. Still, even this prison would be a form of punishment. In most respects, this prison would still be a place where convicted criminals are locked up until they've served enough time for their release. Presumably you wish you had a personal chef and a masseuse, but you wouldn't be willing to go to prison to get them. A punishment that people are excited about experiencing and lining up to try isn't really a punishment at all. Had Dean returned from Hell without any emotional scars, that would have indicated that either Dean is very twisted or that Hell was not the punishment that we think. A mash-up of Ruby's own words remind us that Hell is all bad: "there's a real fire in the pit, agonies you can't even imagine," so "they got it pretty right, except for all the custom leather."

Who the Hell Do You Think You Are?

Our attitudes toward the experience of punishment highlight an interesting feature about Hell in *Supernatural*—a person in Hell might not be there because they lived a bad life, but because they made a really bad deal with a demon. If a soul ends up in Hell this way, does it really deserve this endless torture and suffering? Does it make sense to think of this soul as really being punished? After all, we don't often think of bad consequences for being stupid, as punishments for stupidity, and selling your soul in this way really is just stupid, not evil.

Typically, we assume that any soul in Hell is evil and deserves to be punished. Likewise, we tend to think anyone locked up in a prison is being punished. No doubt, this is a fairly safe assumption, but it obscures an important feature of Hell and of punishment. Punishment is imposed externally for something that was judged to be wrong, and these features distinguish it from other types of negative consequences that stem from things like stupidity. There are choices we make in our lives that have bad consequences, and then there are choices we make in or lives that we are held accountable for through externally imposed bad consequences. Prisoners in a prison are forced to be there for breaking a law and, typically, we think of souls in Hell as being forced to be there for evil actions on Earth.

Of course, making judgments to punish others requires that we have some standards or measures by which we can decide whether or not someone's actions warrant punishment. Furthermore, we take it for granted that a person being punished was made aware that there would be consequences to their actions, prior to making their bad choices. The judge, whoever or whatever that is, balances these factors against the gravity of the offense. And it's common for us to excuse some bad behavior because of a poor upbringing or other mitigating circumstances. So perhaps the final arbiter of Hell takes similar concerns into account. Deals with demons don't fit comfortably in this account. Anyone who really knew what they were signing up for wouldn't make these deals in the first place. Of course, no one ever said there couldn't be really bad consequences for bad choices. Thus, if you're in Hell for something stupid you did, you're not being punished. Rather, you're experiencing the bad consequences of a bad choice.

To Hell with You

Traditionally, the path to Hell is through punishment for failing to meet standards one was aware of. For the sake of justice there need to be exceptions for bad actions done by accident or out of ignorance. The philosopher Joel Feinberg (1926–2004) points this out when he critiques the generally inadequate definitions of his predecessors and contemporaries.[1] According to Feinberg:

> When these articles go on to *define* "punishment," however, it seems to many that they leave out of their ken altogether the very element that makes punishment theoretically puzzling and morally disquieting. Punishment is defined, in effect, as the infliction of hard treatment by an authority on a person for his prior failing in some respect.

As Feinberg sees it, his predecessors and contemporaries left out an important element in their definition, so that it ends up applying to far too many cases that aren't really punishment, including punishing people for breaking rules they didn't know existed.

Feinberg also had some other important examples to consider regarding punishment. Suppose Dean is refused an adult libation at a restaurant, because he failed to bring identification that showed he was legally old enough to purchase and consume adult libations. Has the bartender just punished Dean? No, of course not. Dean didn't do anything wrong and the bartender did not mean to inflict negative consequences on him. On a similar note, suppose you are a high-school athlete and your coach runs you through physically excruciating and exhausting drills at practice. If the coach's intention is to improve your deficient play and conditioning, then this isn't punishment no matter how unpleasant it may be.

These cases aren't cases of punishment, because real punishment is intended to send a message. As Feinberg says:

> Punishment is a conventional device for the expression of attitudes of resentment and indignation, and of judgments of disapproval and reprobation, either on the part of the punishing authority himself or of those "in whose name" the punishment is inflicted. Punishment, in short, has a *symbolic significance* largely missing from other kinds of penalties.[2]

Feinberg's point is that punishment is more than just harsh treatment for breaking rules. In addition, punishment is intended to send a message of moral condemnation to the rule breaker. A true punishment will capture and express the emotional frustration, resentment, and indignation felt by those who support and enforce the rule. Hence, we are frustrated when we follow the rules, while others do not, and we want them punished for their behavior. We want it expressed to them that their actions are offending our moral sensibilities.

Now we can see why going to Hell for stupid choices can't be a punishment. A punishment should send a message of condemnation for the person's failure. But in the case of ignorance, it is not that the person failed to follow a rule. Rather, it is that they didn't know there was a rule to follow. People say that ignorance is no excuse, but when you honestly didn't know you were doing something wrong, you certainly don't see any reason for being punished. You may, after all, recognize your mistake, and never make it again. Knowing this will not get anyone out of Hell if they made a deal with a crossroads demon. But at least those people can take some small comfort in the fact they are not being punished. They're just experiencing the consequences of a bad decision, perhaps one made in partial ignorance.

Hell in a Hand Basket

By all accounts, Hell is pretty bad. But as we've learned, being bad isn't enough for something to count as punishment. In addition to being bad, Hell must be a place where souls go because their past actions failed to follow some set of rules or expectations. These expectations must be such that failure to meet them generates a degree of resentment or indignation on the part of the creators and supporters of the expectations. Ultimately, the punishment tends to mirror the degree of resentment had by those enforcing it, which helps explain why we avoid punishing in the cases where a rule or expectation is not adhered to accidentally. Feeling resentment for an accident is like being angry with a tornado or a werewolf. Sure, they can do a lot of damage, but you really shouldn't take it so personally. Besides, whoever heard of punishing a tornado? And when Sam or Dean put a werewolf down, it would be odd if they were righteous when they did so.

It's important to note from this that, when people don't follow laws, the harshness of their punishment corresponds with the seriousness of the laws they break. Breaking minor laws results in minor punishments, because the overall condemnation for the act is minor. The amount of resentment determines the nature and degree of punishment, not the seriousness of the law that's broken. In "Tall Tales," Dean makes this point clear in a conversation with Sam:

SAM: You know, how would you feel if I screwed with the Impala?
DEAN: It'd be the last thing you ever did.

The severity of the punishment mirrors the seriousness of the act. The consequences of that act are often ignored if they are good and, at worst, used as a reason to increase the punishment if they are bad. Messing with the Impala is obviously something that Dean is very sensitive to, hence the very harsh punishment that he'd bring down upon any offenders. If, as Meg suggests, Hell is the worst possible thing, then going there as punishment would mean having done something very, very offensive to the ultimate arbiter.

Not a Chance in Hell

At the outset I made a point of saying that making a deal with a crossroads demon just doesn't make sense. Nothing is worth eternal damnation. Sure, we see Mary, John, Dean, and Sam willingly trade eternal damnation for seemingly admirable things, but do they really understand what Hell is going to be like? Based on accounts of Hell from Meg and Ruby, it just seems impossible that they could. In "Malleus Maleficarum," Ruby explains:

> There's a real fire in the pit, agonies you can't even imagine ... sooner or later Hell will burn away your humanity. Every Hell-bound soul, every one turns into something else. Turns you into us.

What kind of hunter would choose this if they could avoid it? What kind of person would choose this if they could avoid it? Since Hell is apparently worse than the worst thing we can imagine, then nothing, except the best thing possible would make going there worth it. Of course, if we reason this way, the best thing possible is definitely going to have to be, in part, not having to go to Hell. Therefore, anyone choosing Hell simply has no idea what they've really chosen.

Given Hell can't be something we knowingly choose, we ought to consider whether it's remotely fair to impose it on people for bad behavior. In other words, we need to consider what would justify the existence of Hell as a punishment. Of course, we understand why we punish. We get mad at people when they break rules, and we want to do something harsh in response. But surely we know there are limits to how harshly we can respond to people who commit wrong acts, and further, we recognize that acting out our anger and frustration in these ways isn't our only option. We have a choice about whether or not we punish rule breakers, and as we've already seen, there are cases where we think punishment is unnecessary or unreasonable.

Let's consider something we're all familiar with, punishment for children, to get a better understanding whether or not Hell is justifiable. What is an appropriate punishment for a child who pulls a sibling's hair? Should we pull their hair back, or should we have them sit quietly in "time-out" for five minutes? Either way, what's the real point of these punishments? What do parents hope to accomplish?

Clearly, the punishment is intended to teach some sort of lesson, which is why some parents feel obligated to punish their children. The founder of modern utilitarianism, Jeremy Bentham (1748–1832), recognized the mixed feelings we have toward punishment, saying:

> The general object which all laws have, or ought to have, in common, is to augment the total happiness of the community; and therefore, in first place, to exclude, as far as may be, every thing that tends to subtract from that happiness: in other words, to exclude mischief.
>
> But all punishment is mischief: all punishment in itself is evil. Upon the principle of utility, if it ought at all to be admitted, it ought only to be admitted in as far as it promises to exclude some greater evil.[3]

In essence, regardless of our good reasons for punishing, it still entails our having to subtract from the happiness of the person we're punishing. And of course, we should only do this if doing so is going to prevent some worse evil from happening in the future.

So when it comes to punishing a child for pulling the hair of a sibling, it should only be done, according to Bentham, if doing so will prevent some worse thing from happening in the future. Typically, we expect that our punishing a child will teach them the lesson that they should not pull their sibling's hair in the future. But if we can teach this lesson without punishment, then we must. If punishment isn't effective in preventing a child from getting into greater mischief later, then the punishment is not justified.

Views like Bentham's are utilitarian views because they justify punishment only insofar as the punishment increases the overall amount of happiness for those involved. Generally speaking, the act of punishing is inherently bad, but there are positive consequences in terms of deterrence and rehabilitation for the offender. There may even be positive consequences in terms of the enjoyment felt by the victim of the hair pulling.

That may be all well and good for raising children, but what good comes from punishment in Hell? I think we can easily exclude it as a place of rehabilitation, since nothing seems to leave there in better shape than when it arrives. Given the irrational nature of those making deals with demons, we might be inclined to think of Hell as an asylum run by a bunch of psychopaths. Of course, what good could come from that?

The other possibility is that Hell deters us from acting wrongly. In other words, the threat of going to Hell is so bad that we behave ourselves to avoid going there. But there is a problem with justifying Hell's existence this way, which our "deals with demons" examples from *Supernatural* make clear. Hell is ineffective at deterring, because we don't take seriously how bad it really is. And if we're doing bad things because we don't really understand the consequences, then our bad choices can be excused as irrational, temporary insanity.

If, unlike most characters on *Supernatural*, we did take Hell seriously, then Hell would be the perfect and ultimate deterrent. Since nothing could be worse than Hell, nothing could deter better than Hell. Indeed, a Hell we took seriously would be a Hell that had to be empty. Everyone would do whatever they could to avoid going there, since nothing would be worth that risk. But then, what's the point of an empty Hell? Wouldn't it work just as well for us to honestly think there was a Hell, when in fact, there was no Hell at all? Hell's swell ability to deter perfectly undermines the need to actually have a Hell. In the end, utilitarian considerations just aren't going to justify Hell.

As a possible alternative, the punishment of Hell may be justified according to a retributive theory. In *The Critique of Practical Reason*, the philosopher Immanuel Kant (1724–1804) says:

> When someone who delights in annoying and vexing peace-loving folk receives at last a right good beating, it is certainly an ill, but everyone approves of it and considers it as good in itself even if nothing further results from it.[4]

Kant aptly noticed that we approve of someone getting punished when they deserve it. Even if the punishment doesn't lead to any further good in the world, the punishment is justified. A classic example of retributivism comes to us from the *lex talionis*, which is retaliating in like kind and degree for an injury suffered. The *lex talionis* is often used synonymously with "an eye for an eye," since that captures the general idea of retaliating in like kind and degree.

While Kant's point was that we just seem to approve of punishment, it doesn't make it clear what really makes punishment appropriate. So it can help to think of retributivism as justifying punishment in the same way we might justify rewards or payment for work. If I reward my children for good behavior, then the reward is simply because they behaved well. They don't have to ever behave well again to deserve the reward now. If you're hired to do a job and you complete the job, then you're owed payment for your work. If you don't get paid, your reason for demanding payment will be that you deserve it. Similarly, retributivism justifies punishment simply in virtue of what is deserved. Unlike payment, however, people rarely demand that they be punished for their wrong actions. But, odd though it may sound, according to Kant and other retributivists, you actually have a right to be punished, because punishing you takes seriously your ability to make choices for yourself. Failure to punish you would be like treating you as though you were a little child who can't fully fathom the implication of their actions.

Therefore, when demons claim your soul as payment for granting your wish, they're really just respecting your ability to make your own choices for your life. Likewise, if you are condemned to

Hell because you're a bad person, that too honors your right to be punished, takes your choices seriously, and treats you with dignity. If you've made deals, you need to honor them, and if you've intentionally made wrong choices, then you can expect to be held accountable. But in any case, could you honestly expect that your deals and wrong choices would lead to Hell?

As a punishment, Hell cannot be justified by retributivism. Retributivism justifies giving you what you deserve, but what could you have done in a limited mortal life to deserve eternal suffering? Clearly, if we're going to be treated in like degree and kind, the suffering in Hell needs to be turned down a couple notches or the time spent there shouldn't be without end. When Crowley takes over as King of Hell, he makes some perfectly reasonable changes:

CROWLEY: You don't recognize it, do you? It's Hades, new and improved. I did it myself … See, problem with the old place was most of the inmates were masochists already. A lot of "thank you, sir. Can I have another hot spike up the jacksie?" But just look at them. No one likes waiting in line.

CASTIEL: And what happens when they reach the front?

CROWLEY: Nothing. They go right back to the end again. That's efficiency.

Not only efficient, this version of Hell seems far more fitting than a pit with fire and unimaginable agonies.

What the Hell?

Without a doubt, Hell is fundamental to *Supernatural*, but it is definitely not a justifiable punishment. In fact, any version of Hell similar to the one here couldn't be justified as a punishment. That doesn't mean Hell couldn't exist. It just means that if it did, either it's not a place souls go for punishment or it is still a place that souls go for punishment, though not justifiable punishment. I'm not particularly comfortable with it either way, but I'm especially not comfortable with the idea that the King of the Crossroads is now the King of Hell (and its interior design), since contracts with him are ironclad and not limited to niceties like being reasonable.

Notes

1. A. Flew, "The Justification of Punishment," *Philosophy* 29 (1954): 291–307; S.I. Benn, "An Approach to the Problems of Punishment," *Philosophy* 33 (1958): 325–341; and H.L.A. Hart, "Prolegomenon to the Principles of Punishment," *Proceedings of the Aristotelian Society* 60 (1959–60): 1–26.
2. J. Feinberg, "The Expressive Function of Punishment," *Doing and Deserving* (Princeton, NJ: Princeton University Press, 1970), 95–118.
3. "Cases Unmeet for Punishment," Chapter XIII of *An Introduction to the Principles of Morals and Legislation.*
4. Immanuel Kant, *Critique of Practical Reason*, trans. Lewis White Beck (Chicago: University of Chicago Press, 1949), 170.

Part Two

LIFE, LIBERTY, AND THE APOCALYPSE

Chapter 6

Try Hell, It's a Democracy and the Weather Is Warm

Dena Hurst

The Book of Job speaks of the Leviathan, telling us that "Nothing on earth is its equal—a creature without fear" (41:33). The philosopher Thomas Hobbes (1588–1679) also spoke of a Leviathan, but he was not referring to an all-powerful beast that could overcome any attempt to catch or kill it. Rather, Hobbes was speaking about a government that unites the collective will of the people into a commonwealth that is so powerful that it can withstand all threats. Based on his experience, Hobbes believed that any government was better than chaos. Furthermore, he believed that every form of government except absolute rule would eventually fall apart. The people must submit to the absolute rule of the Leviathan. For Hobbes—much like God in the Book of Job—obedience and peace go hand in hand. Perhaps you can already see the parallels between Hobbes's ideas and the themes in *Supernatural*. There are so many parallels it's hard to know where to begin. But as the King of Hearts said to the White Rabbit, we shall begin at the beginning and go on till we come to the end.

Supernatural and Philosophy: Metaphysics and Monsters ... for Idjits, First Edition.
Edited by Galen A. Foresman.

The Angels Are Coming, the Angels Are Coming

Our beginning is in the second season episode, "Houses of the Holy," where we learn that one function of angels is to serve as the warriors of God. This is based on an interpretation of Luke 2:9, "An angel of the Lord appeared to them, and the glory of the Lord shone around them, and they were terrified." That an angel would terrify people, rather than fill them with a sense of peace or love, is not what we might expect, but, of course, *Supernatural* often defies our expectations. The terrifying nature of angels is testified to in the third season episode, "The Kids Are Alright," in which Ruby says she is frightened of angels, telling Sam that she has not met one and does not want to.

We the viewers finally meet angels in Season 4, which begins with Dean crawling out of his grave and reuniting with Bobby and Sam. After verifying that Dean is not a demon, shapeshifter, or some other creature, they try to figure out how Dean could have come back to life, especially since he had been in Hell. In the second episode of this season, "Are You There God? It's Me, Dean," they learn that only an angel has the power to, as Bobby describes it to Dean, airlift him out of the hotbox. Subsequently we meet Castiel, who pulled Dean from Hell and who reveals to Dean that Lilith plans to break the 66 seals to bring forth the Apocalypse. The angels have returned to earth to stop her, but they need Dean's help. In later episodes, we meet a number of other angels, including Uriel, Zachariah, and Anna. We also learn about archangels, and specifically, we learn of the archangel, Lucifer, and witness his rise by the end of the season.

Thus begins Heaven's civil war. Lilith breaks the seals to free Lucifer and the angels return to stop his destruction of mankind. This is allowed to happen not merely because it was foretold in the Bible, which Cas humorously notes is wrong in more places than it is right, but because, as proclaimed by both Uriel and Zachariah, God is dead.

Without the absolute and central authority of God, there is no one to command the angels. This puts the angels in what Hobbes called a "state of nature," which is not as idyllic as it sounds. Rather, it is the state of war in which people dwell when there is no government to bring order and peace. Hobbes claimed that people cannot live without a strong central authority to rule over them, which we'll see applies to the angels as well. Hobbes pointed out that all people are basically equal by nature and in the state of nature. This does not mean that all people are alike, or that we don't have our own strengths and weaknesses. Instead, as Hobbes explained it, whatever differences we have balance out. Central to understanding this was Hobbes's claim that the weaker could always vanquish the stronger by using cunning or by joining forces with others. In short, Hobbes thought we were all equal because we could all figure out a way to kill one another if we wanted to.

This idea of equality in Hobbes plays out in the breaking of the seals. Specifically, we see how manipulation can overcome brute strength. The angels are far more powerful than most demons, but what they lack in strength, demons make up in cunning. There are protocols outlining who can break the seals, how they must be broken, and in some cases, a particular order in which they must be broken. Therefore, breaking seals isn't simply a matter of being strong enough to do it. In fact, of the 600 seals that exist, Lilith only has to break 66 of them. But to kick off the whole process Dean must break the first one by becoming a torturer during his time in Hell. This leaves Lilith to break the remaining 65 with the help of others loyal to Lucifer. Managing to get a Winchester to start the process of releasing Lucifer certainly wasn't just a matter brute strength. In fact, Dean didn't even realize he had done it until later in the season. This is just par for the course since the Winchesters stay one step behind Lilith's cunning until the last episode, "Lucifer Rising," in which we learn another reason why she has been so successful in breaking the seals. A group of angels, under the leadership of Zachariah, has actually allowed the breaking of the seals by Lilith so that the Apocalypse could begin, believing that the Apocalypse will finally end the battle between Heaven and Hell. To top it all off, the demon Ruby has made Sam into a hulking beast of demon-hunting power, so that he can finally kill Lilith, which happens to be the final seal. And so, after a season of manipulation to open the 66 seals, the king of all cunning rises to destroy mankind.

For Thine Is the Kingdom, and
the Power, and the Glory

Because everyone is equal in a Hobbesian state of nature, there is equal hope of attaining what is desired. As two people cannot possess the same thing, they will become enemies, competing for what they both want. The angels and the demons desire the same thing—to vanquish the other and rule the earth, owning the souls residing there. Outright war prior to releasing Lucifer would have been too costly to both sides since they are relatively evenly matched, with the greater number of demons balancing the greater strength of the angels. The other problem is that even though the angels would probably win, most of the angels don't want a war. Given this, Zachariah and his contingent trust that once Lucifer is released, the angels will have no choice but to fight. War is inevitable so long as the two sides want control over the Earth.

By their machinations, the angels show that they are as weak and lacking in character as humans are, thereby exhibiting the qualities that Hobbes claimed led directly to such a miserable state of nature. There is, however, another quality that contributes to this miserable state, and that is the need for glory. Hobbes claimed that a thirst for glory pushed people to conquer for silly "trifles, [such] as a word, a smile, a different opinion, and any other sign of undervalue ..."[1] Strange as it may seem, the angels clearly have this desire for glory, too. Just recall that Uriel and Zachariah are not motivated by a love of humans when they work to free Lucifer and bring about the end of the Apocalypse. In fact, in "It's the Great Pumpkin, Sam Winchester," Uriel refers to humans as "mud monkeys." Furthermore, both angels admit to admiring Lucifer for having the chutzpah to stand up to God when he commanded them to venerate humans as his favorite among creation. In God's absence, the angels are motivated to bring about the Apocalypse in order to gain greater power in Heaven, and ultimately, greater power over humans, whom they resent.

Absolute Power

Driven by their nature, people—and angels—cannot live in harmony without a central and absolute authority to keep them in order. For Hobbes, the combination of equal abilities, competition, and the need for glory will make the state of nature nothing more than a state of war. As long as the angels and demons are fighting over the same things, and as long as only one can emerge victorious, war is inevitable.

The state of nature is a war of every person against every person, and by analogy, every angel against every angel. Even while the seals are being broken, there is disagreement among the angels as to how they ought to intercede, if at all. The problem with a state of war, as Hobbes pointed out, is that you cannot trust anyone, because even while your allies may appear to be working with you, they may also be secretly plotting against you. Anyone with half a brain—or whatever angels have—should realize that they need to protect themselves against their allies as well as their enemies.

Throughout the series, Sam and Dean live in a state of war against the creatures they hunt, and often the brothers have been put in a position of having to harm other humans in the process, particularly when exorcising demons. In seasons 4 and 5, we see that the angels, too, are in a similar state of war with one another. Uriel's work as an agent for Lucifer comes to light in "On the Head of a Pin," and in "Sympathy for the Devil," Zachariah's plan to unleash the Apocalypse is supported by the archangels Michael and Raphael, thereby demonstrating their willingness to betray both God and many other angels. Tired of waiting for God to reappear, these rebellious angels are willing to sacrifice their own kind for the sake of their own glory.

These rifts amongst the angels first began when God created humans. Having been created first, angels considered themselves to be superior to humans. After all, there weren't any humans for some time, and so the angels probably thought God really loved them. But eventually, God made man and commanded the angels to revere us. Lucifer questioned God's wishes, and for that God banished him from Heaven. Angered at this, Lucifer tortured and perverted a human soul to create the first demon, Lilith. Punishment for this was imprisonment in the Cage, locked with the 66 seals.

As long as there is a state of war, there is no law. The demons were willing to do whatever it took to free Lucifer. Ruby was willing to kill other demons and to appear as a traitor; Lilith was willing to sacrifice her demonic life. Both demonstrated the extent to which the supporters of Lucifer were willing to go. The demons united in the cause of Lucifer's release were powerful and relentless; they were Legion, as it were. The angels, on the other hand, were a heavenly host divided. There were those angels who, in God's absence, chose to rule in his stead, and there were those who did what they could to obey God's word, even in his absence. This was a division between the angels who were able to hold on to faith in God, and those who felt betrayed by God. Thus, there was a state of war on many fronts.

Escaping the State of War: or Why God Makes a Lousy King

For Hobbes, the state of war is something to be avoided at all costs. It is a life of "continual fear and danger of violent death."[2] The way out was to form a civil society under the rule of a single, powerful, sovereign ruler, the Leviathan. To that end, civil society is formed through a social contract. A social contract is simply a contract among all the people to form a society, but for it to work, every person must give up the absolute freedom they had in the state of nature. Since the state of nature had no laws and no rules, everyone had the freedom to do whatever they wanted, whenever they wanted. The result of this lawless state, as we have seen, is the state of war. Therefore, escape from the state of war and into civil society requires giving up these absolute freedoms, and thereby agreeing to obey some rules and laws. These rules and laws are set by and enforced by the sovereign, the Leviathan.

The social contract can come about in one of two ways. The first is by acquisition, when power is used to force individuals to submit to the sovereign. It's not exactly like a normal contract, where you can decide not to sign on the dotted line, but it's just as effective. The second is through mutual covenant, which means the people voluntarily agree to be ruled by the sovereign. While the God of the Old Testament makes many covenants, he behaves more like a sovereign by acquisition. He is the creator of all, and as such, those he has created are beholden to him for their lives. He did not give his creations a long set of terms and conditions that they could opt out of if they so chose. Instead, God demanded perfect obedience in return for harmony in the kingdom of Heaven. Ultimately, Hobbes felt that protesting against the sovereign was unjust, because to challenge the sovereign was to challenge the foundation upon which the civil society was created. Of course, this is exactly why Lucifer was banished.

However, what makes God a lousy king is not his treatment of the angels. As his subjects, they are duty bound to obey him and not question his authority. This is the price for peace. When Lucifer questioned God's command to love and respect humans, he was effectively challenging God's authority to rule Heaven. To preserve the peace, Lucifer either had to be destroyed or exiled. In other words, God wasn't doing anything unjust or unfair to Lucifer or the other angels when he demanded their utmost obedience. As sovereign, that is exactly what God was owed by his subjects. No, the problem with God, and ultimately what makes him a lousy king, is that he failed to maintain control of everything. He failed to maintain civil society. Hobbes argued that the sovereign could not forfeit its power, since such an act would dissolve the society by returning its members to a state of nature, also known as the state of war. But this is exactly what happened when God vanished from Heaven, making no preparations for his absence and designating no substitute god for the interim.

Without the commanding authority of God, whose rule is absolute, there is no law to govern the actions of the angels and maintain balance between Heaven and Hell. When God was present, he united the will of the angels into an ordered existence, commanding their unquestioning obedience. Under his rule, there was peace. But without God, there was no longer a reason to follow the laws, which resulted in a lawless state.

And in such a lawless state, there is no justice. "The notions of right and wrong, justice and injustice have no place. Where there is no common power, there is no law: where no law, no injustice."[3] In this same passage, Hobbes points out that "force" and "fraud" would actually be great virtues in a state of war. Furthermore, he notes that "justice" and "injustice" are attributes of people living in a society, not solitude. But people in a state of war are constantly living in solitude, since they really can't trust anyone ever. In other words, without God, there is no "right" and "wrong," no "justice" or "injustice."

Last, but not least, God's absence meant there was no rightful ownership of anything. As Hobbes wrote, there is only what each person can acquire through wit or force. Something is owned only as long as it can be protected. Zachariah, Michael, Raphael, and their followers hope that if they are successful in their battle for power, they will reign supreme over Heaven and Earth. To accomplish this, the defeat of the forces of Hell must be final. Only a final and absolute victory over Lucifer would bring an end to the state of nature. These angels merely want to bring back civil society through the supreme rule of Heaven, with or without God. If God hadn't been such a lousy king in the first place, they wouldn't have had to resort to such drastic measures.

Hell Is a Democracy

While Heaven falls into chaos during God's absence, Hell becomes fairly democratic. With Lucifer caged up and out of the picture, demons build a relatively civil society through contracts. This is sovereignty by *institution* as opposed to *acquisition*. Ironically, after God ruled through awesomeness, awe-fullness (pun intended), fear, and trembling, the demons built a civil society through contracts. Hell, like Heaven, is populated with souls. After some torture, those souls can be twisted into demons. As witnessed by Dean's time in Hell, after a period of being tortured, the soul has the option of choosing to take over for the torturer. In so doing, the soul is essentially making a contract to be the "employee of," "servant of," or "property of" whatever demon let them off the rack. Lucifer got the ball rolling with Lilith, and presumably, Lilith kept the process moving by torturing more souls, which tortured more souls, which tortured more souls, and so on. Even though it's basically a pyramid scheme, it is a contractual agreement. These sorts of contracts are also be made in other ways. Crossroads Demons, for example, enter into contracts with willing human participants in exchange for their souls. In "The Real Ghostbusters," we learn that Crowley is Lilith's "right hand man," but he's also the King of the Crossroads. So basically, he's upper management in Hell.

These demonic contracts meet the definition of a Hobbesian covenant and are entered into by both parties in true Hobbesian fashion. The wording of the contracts with the Crossroads Demons requires that the demons grant any wish of the person entering into the agreement in exchange for that person's soul. For Hobbes, the promise of any future commitment must rest on trust that both parties can and will fulfill their obligations. The demons bear the brunt of the risk in giving their wares to the customer, extending that credit until a future date when the soul will be collected. Notably, demons are more than willing to carry out their end of the bargain, whereas humans prove quite reluctant to pay on the due date, even our upstanding Dean Winchester.

In a state of war, this would be an issue, as there is no law, no trust, and no sense of justice to bind the parties to their commitment. But as these contracts are entered into in a civil state, one with rules and means of enforcement, one with justice, the reluctant individual can be made to comply with the promise given. And as Hobbes points out, this is the right thing to do. One of the benefits of civil society is that people are forced to honor contracts. As he says, "covenants, without the sword, are but words and of no strength to secure a man at all."[4]

A lawyer might argue that demonic contracts are manipulative in taking advantage of people's weaknesses and thus should be unenforceable. But Hobbes would counter that the contracts are nonetheless entered into willingly by both parties, and as both parties are able to fulfill the terms of the contracts, they are valid. As the people do agree to sell their souls, their being fearful or sad at the time of repayment does not mean that repayment is not due. Unlike the angels, who are born under God's command, demons choose to become members of Hell. This meets the definition of Hobbes's "commonwealth established by institution," wherein people willingly agree to subject themselves to a sovereign. Though many of the same conditions apply in Hell as in Heaven—strict enforcement of laws and subjugation to the sovereign—at least the subjects in Hell agreed to enter into that state, thereby making Hell pretty damn close to a democracy.

The Leviathan

DEATH: There are things much older than souls in Purgatory. Long before God created angels and man he made the first beasts: the leviathan. Why do you think he created Purgatory? To keep those clever, poisonous things out.
"Meet the New Boss"

It is poetic that Hobbes named his absolute government, Leviathan, after the ancient biblical creature. What Hobbes admired about the Leviathan was its size, its strength, and its impervious defenses. As we read in the Book of Job, "If you lay a hand on it, you will remember the struggle and never do it again! Any hope of subduing it is false; the mere sight of it is overpowering" (41:8–9). Hobbes's Leviathan, like the biblical creature, would be strong enough to withstand all assaults from outside usurpers. And there would be no inner turmoil to weaken it from within the society, either. The unity of wills and the obedience to authority would be unfailing (or grave punishment would be meted out). The purpose of the Leviathan was to live, and in living preserve the lives of those within the state. Doesn't that sound darkly familiar?

The leviathans of Purgatory have a strict hierarchy, and a leader who is in absolute control, Dick Roman. They are many who act at the direction of one. The leviathans follow Dick's orders, supporting the master plan to turn Earth into one giant feeding ground, preserving the lives of the leviathan.

The leviathans are unlike the angels in that the angels lacked a unity of wills. Even when Castiel won the civil war, the level of peace that was present under the rule of God was not restored. God remained absent, and Cas was a pretty terrible replacement. Eventually, Dean kills Dick Roman, and the remaining leviathans are weakened and confused. Lacking the command of a central authority to drive their actions, they were unsure how to carry on. They, too, were pushed back to a state of nature, and so their individual private interests took priority.

Hell, on the other hand, still missing its ruler, Lucifer, has found a suitable replacement in Crowley. Having the most support from his contractually obligated demons, the King of the Crossroads takes over the reins of Hell, running it in the most brilliant and efficient manner. (Souls stand in a single long line for eternity.) He preserves order and seeks to expand his territory, as any good Hobbesian sovereign would.

Crowley for President!

Without the presence of God to command the angels there can be no peace, only a natural state of war. Voltaire (1694–1778) once said, "If God did not exist, it would be necessary to invent him," and with this apparently the angels agree. The fact that even the heavenly host can fall into a Hobbesian state of nature does not bode well for humanity, but maybe that's why business has been so good for the King of the Crossroads. Each demon, after all, has willingly agreed to enter into the civil society of Hell. And given the pyramid-scheme nature of Hell's social contracts, there will never be an absence of the sovereign.

Come to think of it, Crowley was born in Scotland in 1661, just ten years after Hobbes published his *Leviathan*. Surely, he was familiar with the book, which would explain the deftness with which he rapidly organizes Hell after the second fall of Lucifer. Furthermore, given their arrogance, there's no way any angels would bother reading a human's book on social and political philosophy. That's too bad though; they could have learned some valuable lessons. If only they'd listened when God told them to venerate man, they could have learned from Hobbes. So I guess God wasn't being such a lousy king when he left. Since he couldn't get some of his best angels to heed his commands, he was forced to banish himself.

Notes

1. Thomas Hobbes, *Leviathan*, ed. Michael Oakeshott (New York: Touchstone, 1997), 99.
2. Ibid., 100.
3. Ibid., 101.
4. Ibid., 129.

Chapter 7

Hunting the American Dream

Why Marx Would Think It's a Terrible Life

Jillian L. Canode

Sam and Dean Winchester travel the country "killing as many evil sons-of-bitches as [they] possibly can" in the hope that one day they can finally settle down and live "a normal, apple-pie life." They each want the American dream: marriage, family, a house. But fate always seems to keep them from that dream. In the Season 4 episode "It's a Terrible Life," the Winchesters are thrust into an alternate world where they are not hunters, but cogs in a corporate machine. This episode is a demonstration of an overarching Marxist theme in the series: the American dream is impossible, because we are alienated and disconnected from our labor through capitalism. As we'll see, the alternate world in "It's a Terrible Life" not only typifies the broader world of the Winchesters in *Supernatural* but also highlights the fact that the Winchesters' lives mirror in horrific manner a terrible life we're all trapped in. That is, of course, if we properly understand Karl Marx (1818–1883).

Supernatural and Philosophy: Metaphysics and Monsters ... for Idjits, First Edition.
Edited by Galen A. Foresman.
© 2013 John Wiley & Sons, Inc. Published 2013 by John Wiley & Sons, Inc.

The Specter of Marx and *Supernatural* Capitalism

Our ability to labor and produce things we enjoy is uniquely human. Unlike animals, we produce simply because we can, not necessarily because we must. We build, we write, we fix up old Chevy Impalas, we make homemade EMF detectors, and we do all of these things for their own sake. We do them because we enjoy the work and because we take pride in our labor. However, when we work merely as a means to survive, we become alienated from ourselves, from our work, and from our fellow human beings. If Dean had a choice between fixing up his beautiful Chevy Impala or working all day everyday on other people's cars just to make a living, Dean would probably choose dying of starvation working on his own Impala over taking a job as a mechanic. Working just to survive takes the pride and enjoyment out of the labor. Under capitalism, the sad fact is that jobs are limited; and so we have to compete with each other for work and for our survival, thereby alienating ourselves from each other.

Noticing this problem, Karl Marx sought to educate the working class through the dissemination of his writings. *The Communist Manifesto*, his most famous work, co-authored with Friedrich Engels (1820–1895), was originally intended as a pamphlet to be spread among workers, explaining the insidious nature of capitalism. As Marx explained, capitalism is an economic system of exploitation. Those who own the companies are the owners of the means of production, and their employees must labor to create marketable products. Selling the products of labor generates massive profits for the owners of the means of production, while the workers earn a subsistence wage. Since people must work for a wage in order to live, they are at the mercy of those who own the companies. If a worker does not like the conditions under which they labor, there will always be another worker who needs a job and is happy to do the work.

One of the fundamental problems Marx saw with the system of capitalism is that labor is no longer something people enjoy, but instead, it is something they loathe. We have to work if we want to survive. Marx explains:

> ... the worker becomes a slave of his object, first, in that he receives an *object of labor* ... he received work; and secondly, in that he receives *means of subsistence*. Therefore, it enables him to exist, first, as a *worker*; and, second as a *physical subject*.[1]

Marx makes clear that because we have to work to pay our rent, pay our bills, and buy our food, work becomes the sole focus of life. Without money we cannot live. Work is primary, making our own humanity secondary.

Capitalism exploits workers, who are disposable and easily replaced. Given this appearance, we might expect the workers to notice the obviously unequal treatment they receive from the owners of the means of production. But, we, the working folk, do not realize the process of selling our labor is dehumanizing, because we just take the work and the system for granted. It is an inevitable part of our lives, or, at least, that is what we are taught and assume. Getting a job in order to live on our own is part of what it means to be an adult. We are expected to graduate from college, get a good job, settle down, and give our parents the grandchildren they always wanted. All of this is how we get true happiness, and none of it is possible without a free-market economy. After all, without capitalism we would not have access to all of the wonderful products we want and need. The American dream is an amalgamation of powerful images indicative of success and happiness. We are led to believe that the new house, the luxury car, the complete collection of *Supernatural* DVDs, and the largest HD television are all items we actually need for an enjoyable life. (And, honestly, the *Supernatural* collection is necessary.) So we work harder, hoping not just to survive but to have enough money left over to buy the things we want for our own enjoyment and to signal to others that we have "made it." Our possessions end up becoming a sign of our level of success.

Capitalism succeeds by selling an image of the perfect life. We spend the majority of our lives working, ticking off the years until retirement, trying to move up in the company, hoping for a big payoff. We do these things because we know there is the great potential to make impressive amounts of money under capitalism. All the while, though, we are blind to the fact that a surplus of money in one place requires a deficit in another. Hence, we buy into and proliferate the propaganda that props up the American dream as something desirable and ultimately attainable.

Within the context of seasons 4 and 5 of *Supernatural*, Sam and Dean Winchester are the laborers, and the angels are the owners of the means of production. Before they meet the angels, Sam and Dean work for themselves, hunting for their own satisfaction and answering to no one. Eventually, however, they realize that to survive the coming apocalypse they will have to labor in the service of someone else. In the interest of saving the world, Sam and Dean agree to help the angels. They learn quickly, however, that angels do not make the best bosses, and really, Sam and Dean have never been very comfortable with authority. Nevertheless, once they are in league with the angels, Sam and Dean believe that they are working toward a time when they will no longer have to hunt. If they just do one more job, they can quit hunting. The semi-unofficial theme song of the show captures it well: "Carry on, my wayward son / There'll be peace when you are done." But in truth, there is no real peace on their horizon, only new obstacles for the Winchesters to overcome, thereby mirroring the life of the worker as Marx saw it. After all, it is in the best interest of the owners of the means of production to keep their workers believing in the possibility of upward mobility, of a time when all the work will be done.

Why It's a Terrible Life

To see why "It's a Terrible Life" works so well as a metaphor for the Winchesters' lives, let's start at the beginning of the episode. In the first scene a hand turns off an alarm clock and the Kinks's "A Well Respected Man" begins to play. This is a song about a man whose dull life focuses on work and success. He goes to and returns from the office at the same time every day, looking forward to the day when he will acquire his father's assets, all the while coveting the girl next door. He is a product of his environment, of his adulterous father, and of his mother who is unhappily married. The well-respected man the Kinks sing about is reminiscent of the kind of person who ends up being a success according the rules of capitalism, which tell us the harder we work the richer we can be.

The episode's title, "It's a Terrible Life," is a play on Frank Capra's classic film *It's a Wonderful Life*, which is in many ways its own warning against the evils of capitalism. Capra's protagonist, George Bailey, saves the people of Bedford Falls from the greedy clutches of Mr. Potter, but not without the help of some angelic inspiration. On the verge of committing suicide, George Bailey is visited by a guardian angel who shows him an alternate world where George never existed, thereby showing George that he is integral to the survival of his community and that his life is wonderful. Similarly, the Winchesters are sent to a world where they are not hunters, but just two unrelated guys who work in the corporate offices of Sandover Bridge & Iron.

As the Kinks play, we see a montage of a day in the life of a person we have come to know and love as Dean Winchester. But this is not *our* Dean. *Our* Dean would not be caught dead in a suit and tie, drinking espresso, eating salads, driving a Prius, and shunning classic rock for NPR. We immediately want to know what happened to the leather coat-wearing, AC/DC-listening, pie-eating, bad-ass who drives a black, '67 Chevy Impala. In this episode, Zachariah, a powerful angel, has created a sophisticated ruse to convince Dean that he can have peace, unfathomable happiness, and lots of women if he sticks to the plan and never quits hunting. It is essentially the same promise capitalism would have us accept in the form of the American dream: Stick to the plan and never stop working, lift yourself up by your own bootstraps and you too can have it all! Of course, the Winchesters' constant failure to get out of the hunting game should be a lesson to us. As long as we buy what capitalism sells, we can never be truly free. Like Sam and Dean locked in a struggle to destroy evil, we are forever locked in a system that will exploit us. The Winchester brothers believe that if they can just eliminate all the ghosts, demons, and other things that go bump in the night, then they can have a normal life. Like us, they are deceived.

Two versions of the American dream are presented in "It's a Terrible Life." The first is presented through the plot of the episode, where Dean is now Dean Smith, a successful man moving up quickly through the ranks of a corporation. In this version of the American dream, Dean experiences the life many business professionals experience, fulfilling the capitalist standards of success. In many ways, this is the apple-pie type of life that Sam and Dean expect when their work hunting is finally done.

Of course, Zachariah doesn't need Dean to long for the pinnacle of capitalistic success. Dean would sell his soul long before he took a corporate desk job. Instead, Zachariah needs Dean to keep hunting, so he cleverly creates a second version of the American dream better suited to fit Dean's personality. This American dream is filled with open roads, cold beers, and delicious cheeseburgers. Since all of these things are far more compelling to Dean, having Dean experience a pseudo-normal corporate life reminds him how lucky he is to be a hunter. Zachariah puts it plainly, "Save people, maybe even the world, all while you drive a classic car and fornicate with women. This isn't a curse. It's a gift." As long as Dean believes that he is in control of his own destiny, he can be used to fulfill the mission of Heaven. While this isn't the American dream that capitalism sells, it is a dream designed to keep Dean in servitude to the Heavenly Host. In order to stay profitable, Corporate America tells workers the same story; it needs the workers to believe they can achieve the dream of the house, car, and family.

No matter how you slice it, "It's a Terrible Life" shows us the absurdity of the American dream through the fiction that is Dean Smith, ironically pursuing an impossible goal that people insist they can reach against all odds. He may be the well-respected man, but as the song demonstrates, the life of the well-respected man does not include anything resembling real happiness. He is overworked and uptight, and he cannot even think about how bad his stock portfolio is. In Season 1's "Hell House," Sam turns to Dean and asks, "Kind of makes you wonder: of all the things we hunted, how many existed just because people believed in them?" Likewise, the idea and ideology of the American dream persists because people believe in it. This fantasy is perpetuated by the few who have in some way become wealthy owners of the means of production and who are employing workers of their own.

The Devil You Now Know

Sam and Dean save the world every season. If they quit hunting, the world in which *Supernatural* is set would literally end. In the Season 2 episode "What Is and What Should Never Be," Dean has a chance to live a normal life with a girlfriend and a job as a mechanic. But he turns away from the opportunity, realizing it is an illusion in which he cannot participate. He opts instead to continue his life as a hunter at Sam's side, because he truly believes the work he does as a hunter is what makes him most human.

Sam and Dean have always believed that they were hunting on their own terms, laboring for its own sake. Seasons 4 and 5 help us realize this belief has been an illusion. Sam and Dean have actually been fulfilling their roles as cogs in a machine they didn't even know existed. "It's a Terrible Life" accurately demonstrates that as long as a system exists wherein the workers are not the owners of the means of production, laboring for its own sake is merely an illusion. The only way out of this *Supernatural* deception is to recognize it for what it really is, and our proletariat protagonists eventually do.

Zachariah's demands of the Winchesters are his ultimate undoing. Marx says, "But not only has the bourgeoisie forged the weapons that bring death to itself; it has also called into existence the men who are to wield those weapons—the modern working class—the proletarians."[2] Maybe Sera Gamble read *The Communist Manifesto* prior to writing this episode, as it so perfectly aligns with the coming events of *Supernatural* after "It's a Terrible Life." Heaven's plan was to use Sam and Dean as mere tools for destroying evil. They were disposable assets, just as the members of the proletariat are disposable to the bourgeoisie.

Just as Marx would have predicted, the boys refuse their roles, choosing instead to strike out on their own, upsetting the heavenly plan. Sam and Dean take control of their lives and fight Lucifer on their own terms. Dean refuses to be the vessel for the archangel Michael, while Sam concedes to being Lucifer's meatsuit, so that he can eventually take both Michael and Lucifer back to the Cage in Hell. Thanks to Sam and Dean, Hell loses and Heaven loses. As the revolutionary Marxist Che Guevara would say, "Hasta la Victoria Siempre," meaning "Until the Eternal Victory."

Can You Handle the Truth?

True to form, this *Supernatural* victory is short-lived, even if it was the Apocalypse. Sam and Dean must return to the fray. Only this time, Dean has had an experience of the normal domestic life, and so he's conflicted about hunting. Ultimately, though, he comes to accept that the American dream, the apple-pie life he temporarily enjoyed, is unrealizable. But if the American dream is unattainable and true happiness can only be achieved through the liberation of the Winchesters as exploited laborers, what would true liberation and a happy life look like for Sam and Dean? Who or what keeps exploiting their labor? No doubt, every fan of *Supernatural* has a theory that forecasts the Winchesters' future, but prophesying happiness for the Winchesters is a tricky business.

As viewers, we think of ourselves as passive, detached, pseudo-participants in their lives. Perhaps, however, we should wonder whether our roles as viewers prevent Sam and Dean from achieving the happiness we want for them. In the grand tradition of the meta-narratives so brilliantly presented on *Supernatural*—including the most meta-episode of them all: Season 6's "The French Mistake"— we should take the meta-analysis one step further and question the blame we the viewers bear in the grand *Supernatural* capitalist scheme.

Sam and Dean Winchester hunt because you and I demand that they do! We watch the show, we buy the DVDs, and we go to conventions. How are we not the same as the bourgeoisie in this scenario? Sam and Dean labor for our enjoyment. They keep hunting because we keep watching them hunt. In "The French

Mistake," Sam and Dean are utterly baffled at the existence of a "bizzaro" universe where people watch them on television.[3] They're equally squeamish about Chuck Shurley's *Supernatural* book series and the LARPing it inspires. We, the fans, play a huge role in the Winchesters' suffering, so it's no wonder we have a hard time imagining a place where Sam and Dean can thrive without hunting. Who would want to watch that?[4]

Notes

1. Karl Marx, *The Economic and Philosophic Transcripts of 1844*, ed. Dirk J. Struik and trans. Martin Milligan (New York: International Publishers, 1964), 109. Hereafter referred to as "Transcripts."
2. Karl Marx and Friedrich Engels, "The Communist Manifesto," in *Karl Marx: Selected Writings*, ed. Lawrence H. Simon (Indianapolis: Hackett Publishing, 1994), 157–186.
3. Many thanks to Galen Foresman for his insight on this point.
4. I would like to acknowledge my gratitude to Abigail Moore; without her I would have never become the *Supernatural* fanatic I am today.

Chapter 8

Mothers, Lovers, and Other Monsters
The Women of *Supernatural*

Patricia Brace

In "It's a Terrible Life," Zachariah tries to convince Sam and Dean that their lives are pretty good, reminding them "You get to save people, all the while you drive a classic car and fornicate with women, it's not a curse, it's a gift." Unfortunately, Zachariah reduces the entire female gender to useful objects, and the Winchesters really are guilty of objectifying women this way sometimes. Still, we shouldn't be too quick to condemn them. A closer look reveals that women play a vital role in shaping and expressing some of the boys' most fundamental moral beliefs.

Kant and Objectification

The philosopher Immanuel Kant (1724–1804) opposed objectification as using a person "merely as a means to an end," and not respecting the person as an end in themselves.[1] Forcing someone to help you do something is using them as a means to achieving your goal or end, because you are not respecting their ability to choose for themselves. According to Kant, our ability to make choices for ourselves is central to being a person, and so by forcing someone to do something, we do not treat them with proper respect.

Supernatural and Philosophy: Metaphysics and Monsters ... for Idjits, First Edition.
Edited by Galen A. Foresman.
© 2013 John Wiley & Sons, Inc. Published 2013 by John Wiley & Sons, Inc.

When fellow hunter, Bobby Singer, does research for Sam and
Dean, he is their tool for acquiring knowledge, but they aren't using
Bobby *merely* as a means. Bobby is not being coerced or forced.
Rather, he's choosing to help out of his loyalty to John and his sons.
As long as he has a choice, he is treated as an individual and not
merely as a means to an end. Essentially, this means Sam and Dean
aren't objectifying Bobby, and further, by letting him choose to help,
they have given him proper respect. This treatment strengthens their
relationships to the point where eventually they're just like family. As
Dean points out to Bobby in "Lazarus Rising," "You're about the
closest thing I have to a father."

By contrast, we see objectification every time a ghost or demon
takes over a human body without permission.[2] After Bobby dies, he
remains in ghostly form to help Sam and Dean defeat the leviathans. In "There Will Be Blood" and "Survival of the Fittest," Bobby
possesses the body of a hotel maid, risking her life in his quest for
personal vengeance. This is a textbook example of objectification.
After almost killing Sam while in this guise, Bobby realizes his mistake, and he decides that it is time to give up the ghost.

The Winchesters and Women

Zachariah's description of a wonderful fornicating life for Sam and
Dean captures some truth but it also misses the importance women
play in shaping the Winchesters' moral decisions. In general,
important women in the lives of Sam and Dean fall into three broad
categories: mothers, lovers, and monsters. Granted, these are not
entirely discrete categories, since lovers and mothers could also be
monsters, but rarely do Sam and Dean relate to a female character
as though she belonged to both categories at once. In "Heart," for
example, Sam's lover, Madison, turns out to be a werewolf. Given
this revelation, Madison cannot remain Sam's lover, and so he puts
her down. Importantly, Madison is not objectified, since it is at her
own request.

Transcending these broad categories is a class of women who are
also warriors. As such, they are soldiers against evil forces, fighting

as equals with Sam and Dean. In a related analogy, Jean Bethke Elshtain discusses the parallel mission of the good soldier and the good mother:

> Some expectations about soldiering and mothering are shared and out in the (cultural) open, so to speak: the soldier is expected to sacrifice for his country as mothers are expected to sacrifice for their children. This isn't quite a sacrificial symmetry, to be sure. Most women do not forfeit life itself but they forfeit a version of what their lives *might have been*, as do male combatants who are forever changed by what they have been through. Uniting the two experiences are *duty* and *guilt*. The soldier and the mother do their duty, and both are racked by guilt at not having done it right or at having done wrong as they did what they thought was right.[3]

Since many of the mother figures to Sam and Dean are also warriors, these women do double duty as soldiers, according to Elshtain. This makes them twice as likely to sacrifice themselves for others; often forcing them to reconcile their own needs with what they feel is their duty. Sam and Dean respect these women most, especially their actual mother, Mary.

The Warrior Mother

Mary Winchester makes only eight appearances on the show, but the memory of her impacts the run of the series.[4] Initially, she is portrayed merely as a helpless victim, the motivation for John's lifelong hunt for her killer. She is the domestic mother who perfectly loves and cares for her family, sacrificing herself to save six-month-old Sam from Azazel.

Mary is an archetypal good mother, but she is also a warrior. When Dean is sent back in time to Kansas of 1973, he is shocked to find that it was not his father's family who were hunters, but his mother's. In a continuation of their role reversal, John is put in the traditional ingénue position when he is brutally killed and used by the demon to blackmail Mary. Azazel makes her an offer she can't refuse: not only will he bring John back to life, but "You'll be done with hunting forever, white picket fence, station wagon with a coupla kids, no more monsters or fear." Mary knows she's alone without John, and he's her ticket out of hunting.

In this instance both Mary and Azazel objectify John, using him for their own means without his knowledge or consent. He is the bargaining chip, and by consenting to the deal, Mary wins back his life and a ticket out of hunting. In exchange, she sacrifices another person's life without their consent, Sam. In effect, Mary gets the standard ten years for being willing to sacrifice Sam, so that her lover could live and she could have a normal life. In one fell swoop, the warrior mother objectified her lover and son, and Dean saw the whole thing.

Ellen Harvelle embodies what Mary could have been had she survived. She is a tough, capable, resourceful business owner, running Harvelle's Roadhouse, which serves as an important meeting place for hunters. If Bobby is like a father, then Ellen and her daughter Jo are the rest of their surrogate family. Ellen accompanies Bobby and the brothers on important missions, including joining them at the Devil's Gate, "When All Hell Breaks Loose, Part 2." There, the demon Azazel objectifies her, using her to make the men back-off by forcing her to point a gun at her own head. This wouldn't have been possible, except for the loyalty and respect that Sam, Dean, and Bobby have for her.

In "Abandon Ye All Hope," Ellen gives her life to help Sam and Dean. Jo is already badly mauled, and knowing that her daughter won't make it, Ellen stays with her to ensure that the building is destroyed while she's still inside. In another sign of respect, Sam and Dean accept her self-sacrifice, even though it robs them of another warrior mother.[5]

Sam and Dean have idealized their short time with their mother, thinking of her love as pure and unconditional. Their simultaneous resentment and respect for their father is due in large part to the fact that he obsessively searches for her killer, robbing them of an ordinary domestic life. As a result, Sam and Dean struggle to adopt values they think their mother wanted to instill in them. This unique feature of their heroic quest balances the strong "homosocial" relationships Sam and Dean form with other men in the show.

Homosocial relationships are relationships in which the primary social bond is with someone of the same gender. We see these relationships among men in the heroic epics of antiquity, like the *Odyssey*, *Iliad*, and *Aeneid*, as well as other popular genres like westerns, war films, and road pictures. The hero's gender in these stories is almost always male, and his closest relationships are with other males, like Tonto, Sundance, Robin, Watson, Chewie, Woody, and Silent Bob. These homosocial couple relationships often supersede the hero's heterosexual romances, which play second fiddle to the "men's work."

Growing up without their mother has left Sam and Dean without some of the basic practical knowledge they need to enter a committed loving relationship with a woman. As far as they know, Mary was the love of their father's life, and her death set him off on his quixotic quest.[6] Without a visible working model of a real marriage, it's no wonder Dean tends to objectify women. It's almost miraculous that Sam is able to break the homosocial bonds of Dean and John to settle down with Jessica, even for a short time.

Lovers, Utilitarianism, and the Mission

According to the philosopher John Stuart Mill (1806–1873) "right" and "wrong" are based on how much good results from one's actions. Good consequences count more than an individual's right to decide for themselves.[7] In other words, the needs of the many outweigh the needs of the few.[8] Sam and Dean are all too familiar with this philosophy of utilitarianism. Many times they have sacrificed relationships with women for the sake of their mission. Women represent hearth and home to Sam and Dean, things they're used to giving up for the greater good.

Sam leaves Jessica, and later, Dean leaves Lisa. Both boys view these break-ups as necessary to achieving what's really important. Granted, Sam would like to return to Jessica, but Azazel prevented that. This is enough to show that Sam and Dean think their primary contribution to the world is hunting. Still, we should note that while Sam and Dean often objectify others to obtain their ends, they don't value themselves more highly. They see themselves as tools, just like the next person.

This thinking is brought clearly into relief when Sam or Dean is removed from hunting. In "What Is and What Should Never Be," Dean dreams of a perfect life, settled, and with a girlfriend, Carmen. Sam is in law school, engaged to Jessica, and their mother is still alive. Both brothers have a female partner, and everything is pleasantly domestic. Dean revels in domestic tasks, like mowing the lawn, complete with a lawn gnome, flowers, and a white picket fence. Ironically it is his very happiness with mundane drudgery that helps Dean figure out that this is a false reality. Visiting his father's grave punctuates the deep schism between his need for a domestic life and his need to sacrifice himself entirely to the mission. Knowing his father would tell him his happiness isn't worth the lives of so many others, Dean asks, "Why do I have to be some kind of hero? Why do I have to sacrifice everything, Dad?"

Later, in talking with Sam, he's still trying to make sense of his own self-worth. Dean says, "All I can think about is how much this job has cost us." Sam, having dealt with these questions for a long time, tries to help, "It's not fair. It hurts like Hell, but it's worth it."

Sam and Dean Self-Esteem

When the brothers are apart a more grounded domestic state becomes possible. When Sam goes to Hell at the end of Season 5 and Dean is left to continue without him, Dean ends up in a domestic situation with another old flame, Lisa Braedon, and her son, Ben. When Dean goes to Hell at the end of Season 3 and to Purgatory at the end of Season 7, Sam likewise enters into domestic situations. He forms an alliance with the demon Ruby in Season 3, who becomes his mentor and sexual partner, and in Season 8 he connects with a female veterinarian, Amelia, and a dog, the traditional symbol of family loyalty, which he literally runs over.

When the brothers are given different non-hunter lives in "It's a Terrible Life," Sam tells Dean he knows that he is meant for something better than this. But tellingly, neither brother has a domestic love relationship in this scenario. It seems easy enough to feel like your life could have more value when you don't share it with others. And of course, these lives are an illusion, designed by Zachariah to manipulate Sam and Dean into feeling like their hunting lives have meaning. As we noted at the beginning of this chapter, Zachariah reminds them, "You get to save people, all the while you drive a classic car and fornicate with women, it's not a curse, it's a gift." So Zachariah blatantly objectifies women in order to use, or objectify, Sam and Dean.

Throughout *Supernatural* the objectification of the Winchesters is contrasted with a happy domestic life. Sam and Dean are mistaken in thinking that their only value resides in the roles they play in the larger battles of good and evil; if they looked deeper they would see that they both would prefer a loving relationship with a woman. It's only supernatural evil and the lives of thousands of innocent people that force them to repeatedly sacrifice the lives they'd prefer.

But Sam and Dean Are So Pretty

Objectification isn't just a one-way street, and so *Supernatural* includes a great deal of objectification of men *by* women. When we first meet Meg Masters in "Scarecrow," she's a cute, petite blonde, and an utterly fearless hitchhiker. But we quickly see Meg's true form when she uses men for rides and blood sacrifices. In opposition to Kantian ethics, she sees them as having *instrumental* value only, using them the same way we would any other tool, as merely a means to an end.

"Shadow" gives us another example of objectification, with Meg using Sam and Dean to bait John Winchester into revealing himself. While the brothers are tied up, Meg sits on Sam, caressing his body, and kissing him against his will. While Meg is busy with Sam, we see Dean using a hidden knife to saw through his bindings. Not trusting Dean, Meg checks on him, finds the knife, and mocks Sam for trying to distract her. Then, in a somewhat satisfying moment, Sam reveals that he had a knife too.

Given the regularity with which Sam and Dean overcome being objectified by women, it could easily be misconstrued as yet another illustration of male dominance. But it's important to note that virtually every case like this involves a woman in the role of monster, which implies that Sam and Dean's overcoming the objectification is intended as an illustration of good winning over evil, not man over woman. The fact that we almost never see a woman who isn't a monster objectify a man, speaks to the positive moral role women play in the Winchesters' lives. Of course, the one glaring counterexample is their mother, Mary.

In her defense, Meg might argue that she has no choice but to objectify others to achieve her ends. Her duty is to her master, Azazel. Kant argued that we all have duties and the motivation to do one's duty should not be bound up with the consequences. Rather, the only motivation to do one's duty is the simple fact that it is one's duty. Understanding that something is your duty means you've understood that you do it no matter what. What if Meg is just doing her duty? Well, Kant would certainly deny that it is her duty to follow the instructions of a demon. If she believes that it is, then Meg is simply mistaken.

The Conduct of War

The episode "Jus in Bello" highlights the tension between the Winchesters' duty to the greater good, their respect for women, and the value they place on their own lives. Tough decisions are made, giving us a better idea of what's really important to Sam and Dean, morally speaking.

All of the important action in this episode is instigated or orchestrated by women, beginning with the thief, Bela. She has stolen the Colt, and in trying to retrieve it, Sam and Dean are caught in a trap and taken to a local police department in Monument, Colorado. Entering in chains, the brothers have their first encounter with the department secretary, Nancy Fitzgerald, who eyes them suspiciously. Dean quietly says to her as he passes, "We're not the ones you should be scared of Nancy." Dean is wounded in his cell, and an unprompted Nancy goes to check on him, allowing Sam to steal her crucifix to make holy water. Later, after it's clear that Sam and Dean are not the problem, Nancy takes the news that demons are about to attack the building remarkably well.

Shortly after this, the third important woman of the episode arrives, the demon Ruby. Straightaway, she chastises Sam and Dean for not having the Colt, explaining that without it, they have little hope of escaping. A monster woman warrior and some-time lover, Ruby is a force to be reckoned with. So it's not without trepidation that Dean listens to Ruby's proposed solution. They can use a spell that would vaporize every demon in a one-mile radius (including Ruby herself), but there's a catch. This seeming salvation requires the sacrifice of a virgin, which turns out to be Nancy.

Nancy asks what she needs to do for the spell and Ruby bluntly says, "You can hold still while I cut your heart out of your chest." Undaunted, Nancy asks Ruby if by doing so they could save the townspeople outside, most of whom are her friends. The men object to Nancy considering this further, but amidst these objec-tions, Nancy cuts them off, saying "It's my decision."

Dean and Henrikson refuse to accept Nancy's decision, but Sam is willing to consider trading her life for 30 others. Dean objects, saying "So we throw away the rule book and stop acting like humans? I'm not gonna let that demon kill some nice sweet inno-cent girl, who hasn't even been laid. I mean look, if that's how you win wars then I don't wanna win." Sam reluctantly agrees, and they develop an alternate plan for survival, which ultimately fails for everyone but Sam and Dean.

Dean's comments show a conflicted system of values. He wants people to survive, but he's not willing to kill one innocent person to achieve that goal. And Henrikson's line, "We don't sacrifice people. We do that, we're no better than them," echoes Kant's view that humanity holds a special place because of the free choices it can make. However convincing these expressions of Kantian moral values may be, it's not clear that they actually motivate Dean. Because if Dean was truly motivated by Kant, why would he ignore Nancy's free choice? Or is free will just for Dean Winchester?

It's difficult to tell what respect Dean has for Nancy, despite all that she's done and is willing to do. Here, Dean's explicit reasoning is pretty selfish. He doesn't want to live in a world where some sweet innocent girl is sacrificed to save the lives of dozens of others. Sam, on the other hand, is forced to select between two entirely different moral concerns. So Nancy's willingness to sacrifice herself gives us different insight on his moral concerns. Where Dean isn't willing to respect Nancy's right to make decisions for herself, Sam is. Sam is also willing to live in a world where sacrificing an innocent person to save dozens more, while not ideal, makes some sense.

Ultimately, Sam's decision is motivated by either his loyalty to Dean or Dean's actual argument, but it's unclear. Of course, it would have been dramatically out of character for him to insist on Nancy's death, especially if she hadn't volunteered. While Sam understands utilitarian reasoning, his actions more often fit with his Kantian duties.

And Other Monsters

Given what we've discovered so far, I wonder how the scenes in "Jus in Bello" would have gone if it turned out that, unbeknownst to her, Nancy was a virgin werewolf. Would Dean have given that tear-jerking speech? If Nancy had refused to be sacrificed, would Dean have forced her to be sacrificed? Would Sam have tried to stop him?

The relation of monsters to Sam and Dean is always tenuous, but it's made far more so when the monster is a woman. Typically, a monster is only allowed to live if it serves to benefit Sam and Dean. In this respect, monsters are already objectified, but there are occasions where a few female monsters have risen slightly above this status, if only temporarily.

In "The Slice Girls," Dean has some very unwise unprotected sex with Lydia, an Amazon who picks him up in a bar. The Amazons are a tribe of women who made a deal with the Greek goddess Harmonia for supernatural power in return for sacrificing the fathers of their daughters. Dean's Amazon child, Emma, ages to teendom in less than two days. Arriving out of the blue, she explains to Dean what she is and that she needs his help to leave the tribe. Dean is compassionate, but it turns out that Emma's sob story is a ruse to kill him. The episode concludes with Sam killing Emma before Dean has to.

Similarly, in "The Girl Next Door," Dean kills the kitsune, Amy. While not Sam's monster daughter, she was a monster that Sam befriended as a child. Amy had even saved Sam's life by killing her own mother. When Sam kills Dean's daughter, he believes he is saving his brother's life. To some degree, the fact that Emma was a monster didn't play much of a role in the killing. It was only an important factor to help Dean understand and grieve quickly. Dean's killing of Amy is far more baffling. Yes, she's a monster, but she's killing because she's a mother. She's trying to save her son's life, and Dean can certainly relate to that. Otherwise, Amy is a good person, and has even done Dean a favor once, saving Sam. The only explanation can be that Dean is blindly following a sense of duty that he doesn't fully understand.

No Rest for the Wicked

As we've seen, the women of *Supernatural* highlight many of the flaws our heroes have in understanding what they themselves actually value. Sam and Dean don't just fornicate with women. Truly, they value women more than they realize or admit. Despite their commitment to their duty of saving people and hunting things, Sam and Dean sometimes glimpse that there is more to life. In fact, they risk objectifying themselves by using themselves merely as tools to fight monsters and demons. If they ever fully realize this, we'll have to find another dynamic duo to save the world.

Notes

1. Immanuel Kant, *Groundwork of the Metaphysic of Morals*, ed. Thomas E. Hill Jr., trans. Arnulf Zweig (New York: Oxford University Press, 2003).

2. Angels seem to be the only ones limited to having to ask permission before they can take over a human's body.

3. Jean Bethke Elshtain, *Women and War* (New York: Basic Books, Inc., 1987), 222.

4. She appears as a young mother during flashbacks in the Pilot and "All Hell Breaks Loose, Part 1" (Season 2, Episode 21); as a ghost, "Home" (Season 1, Episode 9); as Sam's hallucination, "When the Levee Breaks" (Season 4, Episode 21); in two time travel episodes "In the Beginning" (Season 4, Episode 3) and "The Song Remains the Same" (Season 5, Episode 13); as a dreamed flash forward, "What Is and Never Will Be" (Season 2, Episode 20); and as a seemingly out of place sex object to the angel Zachariah in Heaven, "Dark Side of the Moon" (Season 5, Episode 16).

5. Mothers and self sacrifice are a recurring theme in the series, for example in the Season 7 episode "What's Up Tiger Mommy," the new prophet Kevin Tran's mother Linda is willing to sell her soul to obtain her son's freedom.

6. They do learn later that John fathered another son, their younger half-brother Adam, in Season 4, Episode 19, "Jump the Shark."

7. John Stuart Mill, *Utilitarianism* (Indianapolis: Hackett, 2002).

8. Charles Dickens, *A Tale of Two Cities* (New York: Washington Square Press, 1965), and also famously quoted by Mr. Spock in *The Wrath of Kahn* (1982).

Chapter 9

Night of the Living ~~Dead~~ Demons and a Life Worth Living

John Edgar Browning

Supernatural fans often associate Season 3's popular "Jus in Bello" episode with the world's quintessential zombie movie, George Romero's *Night of the Living Dead* (hereafter *Night*). There are no plodding zombies, but the "massification" of demons in the episode is a clear allusion to *Night*.[1] In addition to the massification, there is a second element that firmly situates this episode among other Romero-inspired works, namely a "survival space," a central enclosure in which one's personal and collective actions against the massing monsters outside are made central to the story. In fact, it was not Romero's *Night* but Richard Matheson's novel *I Am Legend* that actually originated the survival space.[2]

But even though Romero's *Night* didn't conceive the survival space, it did perfect it. Romero's zombie films, beginning with *Night*, fill the survival space with multiple, diverse survivalists who are forced to work through personal differences stemming from jealousy and petty annoyance to racism and bigotry, issues of morality, theology, and other social and cultural differences. Failure to do so often comes at a very high price—the group's gruesome demise. This change from *I Am Legend* (hereafter *IAL*) is wildly important, because it lends Romero's film, sequels, and offshoots their "most fundamentally entertaining and dramatic qualities,"[3] whereby *whether* one survives pales utterly in significance to *how* one survives or dies.

Supernatural and Philosophy: Metaphysics and Monsters ... for Idjits, First Edition.
Edited by Galen A. Foresman.
© 2013 John Wiley & Sons, Inc. Published 2013 by John Wiley & Sons, Inc.

These motifs not only fundamentally link "Jus in Bello" to Romero's *Night* and Matheson's *IAL*, but they help fuel the episode's continued popularity. Furthermore, the episode extends the conventional and cultural markings of its predecessors by modifying a formula that is generally restricted to straight zombie narratives. In the end, we find that the multi-defended survival space in "Jus in Bello" plays the same role it did in Romero's films, despite its shift away from zombies to demons. "Jus in Bello" creates a politically charged space in which progressive and conservative social and cultural elements are repeatedly tested, negotiated, and replaced. This continuous circulation of political conflict affords zombie narratives their sustained entertainment and cathartic qualities.

A Night to Remember

In "Jus in Bello," Sam and Dean are hot on the trail of the thief Bela to retrieve the stolen Colt. Having tracked her to Monument, Colorado, the brothers find her motel room empty. Unfortunately for the Winchesters, they have walked into a trap. After the local police storm into the room, Sam and Dean are confronted by their old adversary Special Agent Victor Henricksen. Once they're taken into custody at the local sheriff's office, the small town setting is clear. Of course, small towns certainly aren't out of place in *Supernatural*, but the fact that nearly the entire episode takes place in the small, cramped enclosure of a police station is unique. Indeed, the setting is the first link to Romero's *Night*, whose cramped Pennsylvanian farmhouse is little different than the poorly fortified police station holding Sam and Dean.

Agent Henricksen is bent on keeping Sam and Dean in custody, since he has been burned by the capture and loss of the Winchesters before. To reduce the risk of escape, Henricksen quickly phones his superior, Deputy Director Steven Groves, who immediately boards a helicopter bound for Monument to hasten Sam and Dean's expedition. The Winchesters are marched into a small holding cell to wait for the arrival of Groves.

Upon his arrival, Groves insists that Henricksen complete an inordinate amount of paperwork, thus allowing Groves to visit Sam and Dean, revealing himself as a demon and shooting Dean in the shoulder. Sam quickly tries to exorcise Groves, but he's interrupted by the demon saying, "Sorry, I gotta cut this short. *It's gonna be a long night, fellas!*" and abandoning Groves's dead body. After discovering Groves, Henricksen is reluctantly convinced that Sam and Dean had no part in his death, but he refuses to believe Groves was possessed.

The demon's foreboding words, "*It's gonna be a long night, fellas!*" is a telltale hallmark of Romero's *Night*. "Jus in Bello" plays out over the course of a night, and the troubles to come are foreshadowed shortly after when another agent, Calvin Reidy, discovers the helicopter pilots' throats have been slashed. As though that weren't enough, the helicopter explodes and Reidy is killed by one of the fallen officers whose body has been possessed by a demon. Everything goes to Hell very quickly, almost shockingly so (even for *Supernatural*); this is unmistakably reminiscent of *Night*, including the bodies strewn everywhere. The local sheriff is thrown into a state of panic and urges everyone to go outside and flee. The wiser Henricksen, convinced they are under siege, implores everyone to stay inside and barricade the doors. This is precisely the course of action suggested by Romero's protagonist, Ben, in *Night*. Furthermore, the office secretary, Nancy Fitzpatrick, quickly discovers that all modes of communication with the outside world are out. Her revelation, "The internet, my cell, it's all dead. How can it all be dead?" parallels that of her counterpart Barbra from *Night*, who pleads hysterically and repeatedly with Ben, "What's happening? What's happening? I don't understand what's happening!" In only a few gruesome and explosive moments, Sam and Dean are trapped in the station with a handful of survivors.

When Is a Choice Not a Choice?

Terrifyingly—but right on cue—the power goes out, another scene right out of *Night*. Sheriff Dodd beseeches everyone to leave, but

Henricksen yells, "Nobody's going anywhere! Everybody just calm down!" Already, the differences among individuals are emerging in the survival space. Dodd pleads for the lives of the men outside, but without hesitation Henricksen explains that they're all dead, along with whoever else goes outside. Henricksen tells the sheriff and deputy to lock the windows and bar the doors, and while they do, he reassures Nancy, saying, "I'm gonna get you through this, you got my word. You got that?" Henricksen has effectively taken charge of the survival space, just as Ben's character did in *Night*. Henricksen's attire even nuances Ben's, and Barbra's fear and vulnerability in *Night* are, in turn, mirrored in Nancy. Even the gender and racial diversity of these particular couplings are matched.

Henricksen frees Sam and Dean from their cell, asking, "How do we *survive*?" Their initial solution follows lock step with *Night*. They fortify the jail from demons with devil's traps and salt, rather than the wood and nails needed for zombies (see Figures 9.1 and 9.2). Dean unsuccessfully attempts to retrieve some weapons from the Impala, foiled by a mass of demons in columns of black smoke. Magically barred from entering the station by the salt barriers, the demons fan out to possess 30 or so town locals. In their newly acquired "meatsuits," they return to the station and gaze eerily at the building. Nancy recognizes a friend among the mass of demon meatsuits. "Is that where the black smoke went?" she wonders. "Looks like," Sam replies.

The people outside all have black eyes, devoid of expression. They're demons, seemingly listless and emotionless, but they're actually focused. Of particular significance here is not only the expressionless, zombie-like behavior, but the survivalists' recognition of the humanity still expressed in the bodies and faces of the possessed townspeople. This is the massification of the almost-human, used by Romero and Matheson to highlight and indict the potential lack of humanity remaining for those left in the survival space (see Figures 9.3 and 9.4).

Safely inside, Dean distributes charms that will protect everyone from possession. As they ready themselves for the siege, Dean and Henricksen engage for the first time in friendly

Figure 9.1   "Jus In Bello"—Jared Padalecki as Sam in *Supernatural* on the CW television network

Figure 9.2   Duane Jones as Ben defending the farmhouse behind boarded windows in *Night of the Living Dead* (1968)

Figure 9.3   "Jus in Bello"—Massing demon-possessed townspeople in *Supernatural* on the CW television network

Figure 9.4   Massing zombies in *Night of the Living Dead* (1968)

conversation, finding there is much they share in common. Henricksen asks for the hard truth:

HENRICKSEN: What's out there—can you guys beat it? Can you win?
DEAN: Honestly? I think the world's gonna end bloody. But that doesn't mean we shouldn't fight. We do have choices. I choose to go down swinging.

The plurality of choices here is central. In Matheson's *IAL*, Neville is the lone survivor, defending his home, which is the novel's survival space. That is, at least, until Ruth shows up, and joins him in the survival space. Nearly 15 years after *IAL*, Romero reworks Matheson's framework in a few key ways. By populating the space with multiple people, and by extension, multiple and opposing choices, Romero makes the survival space a repository for social ills, values, and ethics. Romero thus imaginatively recreates a place of defense and fortification into an incubator for a world of many possibilities, forged through the critical self-examination of those within. "Jus in Bello" plays this out as well (see Figure 9.5 and Figure 9.6).

The demon Ruby enters the scene by suddenly crashing through a window where the salt barrier has been compromised accidentally. She comments on getting guts caught in her mouth while fighting her way into the jail, a gory trope common in *Night*. The situation looks bleak. They have no Colt, no major arsenal, nothing. Any foreseeable outcome inspires little hope, and worst of all, Ruby reveals that the onslaught is under the command of the ancient and powerful demon Lilith. An ironic savior, Ruby offers a solution through a spell that will vaporize every demon in the area, herself included. Unfortunately, Ruby's spell requires a virgin sacrifice, and the only virgin around is the secretary, Nancy. Nancy tries to volunteer, saving everyone the difficult deliberation of killing one to save many. However, Dean outright opposes this plan, convinced instead they should just open the doors and fight off the demons as best they can, killing many in order, hopefully, to save one.

The episode's title, "Jus in Bello," refers to the law that governs the way warfare is conducted. In this scenario, their choices are few and simple. The first is to use Nancy's heart to complete Ruby's

Figure 9.5 "Jus in Bello"—Pictured (L–R) in the survival space, Jensen Ackles as Dean, Aimee Garcia as Nancy, Jared Padalecki as Sam, Charles Malik Whitfield as Sgt. Hendriksen, in *Supernatural* on the CW television network

spell, which will eradicate all the demons in a one-mile radius. Though this would kill Nancy, it would save the possessed towns-people. The survivalists discuss the option:

> HENRICKSEN: We don't sacrifice people. We do that, we're no better than them.
> RUBY: We don't have a choice.
> DEAN: Yeah, well, your choice is not a choice.

Sam, on the other hand, supports the utilitarian argument that killing *one* virgin will save *many* of the people inside and outside of the jail. The others simply won't go for it though. Instead, they side with Dean's appeal to the absolute universal law that prohibits killing innocent people, even if sacrificing that *one* person will save the lives of many others. Herein, we have a dramatic clash of values within the survival space. Considering Dean's plan pure suicide,

Figure 9.6   Pictured (L–R) in the survival space, Judith O'Dea as Barbra, Judith Ridley as Judy, Karl Hardman as Harry Cooper, Duane Jones as Ben, in *Night of the Living Dead* (1968)

Ruby leaves, thereby making it clear that she was never really a member of the group. Rather, Ruby has played the role of temptress. As in Romero's movies, so in *Supernatural*: If a conflict of values doesn't arrive from within the survival space, an external catalyst is employed to force the issue.

Meanwhile, the demons are congregating listlessly around the jail. This is an obvious visual homage to the isolated Pennsylvanian farmhouse in *Night*. When the siege finally begins and the demons enter the survival space, we see something we didn't expect. The guns are all loaded with rock salt, serving to incapacitate the demons without killing the townspeople they occupy. But why bother with the incapacitation? If anyone is going to survive, then the demons must die. Attempting to hold true to Dean's absolute moral compass, the survivalists have devised a clever tactical maneuver. Sam, Dean, and Henricksen fight to slow down the demons that have been let inside intentionally. During the fight, Nancy and the deputy reseal the doors from the outside to trap the demons inside. Finally, a pre-recorded exorcism in Sam's voice comes over the office's PA system, sending every last demon inside back to Hell. One fan remarked on a forum that it was, "rather like *Night of the Living Dead* in reverse."[4] This comment refers to the fact that the good guys let the demons inside the station, as opposed to trying to defend it endlessly. The survivalists managed to transform their externally fortified survival space into a cleverly utilized mechanism for escape.

All's Well That Ends Well

Clearly, the survival space lends "Jus in Bello" the same entertaining and dramatic qualities that have allowed post-Matheson zombie films to prosper, infecting even the video gaming industry through the "survival horror" subgenre. But beyond entertainment, what's really the big deal? For many, the unfortunate truth is probably not much. But for those fans paying attention to the political tension that swells and contracts within these survival spaces, the popularity of nearly every sequel, adaptation, or hybrid of these works rests on its ability to flex and evolve that survival space in a new way. The survival space is a testing ground, a proving ground, for beliefs and values and thus "Jus in Bello" is appropriately named for its consideration of what law should govern such warfare.

The resolution of zombie narratives gives each title and era its own unique signature. The classic *Dawn of the Dead* (hereafter *Dawn*), a sequel to *Night*, is a prime example. In *Dawn*, the survivalist group is a mixture of very different kinds of people, much like *Night* and "Jus in Bello." After escaping Pittsburgh by helicopter, this group of survivalists finds itself taking refuge in a shopping mall teeming with zombies. The group works together to retake the mall from the zombie horde, all the while, bearing each other's interests in mind. Facing a common foe, the entire group works in harmony to secure the mall. Unfortunately, having neutralized the common enemy that unified them, the group's true test is learning to live with one another within the survival space. Safely inside the mall, the group returns to a relatively normal consumer life: living, shopping, lavishly drifting idly from one store to the next. Ironically, despite the feast of consumerism at their fingertips, they are listless like zombies. Note that had Dean caved to Ruby's plan, the result would have been the survival of a small group that would have lost some of their humanity too.

According to Gregory A. Waller's important study of horror narratives in *The Living and the Undead: From Stoker's Dracula to Romero's Dawn of the Dead*, "destruction of the undead," the "resumption of normality," and the "concluding sequences," often "question whether normality is worth saving or resuming."[5] For Romero's *Dawn*, in particular, unabated consumerism appears equally as monstrous as the threat outside the survival space. The work of the demons in "Jus in Bello," like the zombies in *Night* and *Dawn*, is ceaseless and instinctual. Lacking the ability to make choices, at least these monsters are blameless for their horrific actions. Therefore, "the living must also work," Waller continues, "to defend themselves, to survive, to protect, and even perhaps to redeem that which they deem most valuable in the world." So even though radical survival methods will remind us, Waller would say, of "what Van Helsing calls [in *Dracula*] the 'wild work' of destruction," we must be careful how that wild work is carried out, recalling Dean's claim that "[Ruby's] choice is not a choice," even if it is a means of survival. Put simply, the "wild work" of survival for Dean involves at minimum continuing a life worth living, which obviously entails a life that doesn't involve killing virgins.

Dénouement: Teaching a Dead Dog, New Tricks

Having managed to achieve the seemingly impossible, saving both the townspeople and the virgin, Sam and Dean say their final good-bye to their former nemesis, now friend, Henricksen. Some time passes and we find Sam and Dean in yet another nondescript motel when Ruby arrives with news:

> RUBY: Lilith killed everyone. She slaughtered your precious little virgin, plus a half a dozen other people. So after your big speech about humanity and war, turns out your plan was the one with the body count. Do you know how to run a battle?

What was seemingly a night to survive, a night to get through as best you could, was actually a whole lot more. Again, the survival space is a testing and proving ground for beliefs and values, wherein resolution gives each zombie adaptation and era its own unique signature. The legacy of these adaptations hinges on how viewers empathize with their characters despite the wholly fantastical world that surrounds them. Even the most shameful behaviors by heroes are sometimes forgiven.

Ruby's scalding indictment is apt. For the narrow space of a night, Henricksen and the Winchesters managed to survive in such a way that they could live with their choices. But had they not been so selfishly concerned with how they could live with themselves after the night had ended, they could have honored Nancy's free choice to save them all. Of course, that would mean giving up on being the macho heroes and letting a girl do it for them, but ultimately the result would have been far better. This is the unique signature of "Jus in Bello," and it says a lot about Sam and Dean. But it may say even more about the viewers who enjoyed it and the world they live in.[6]

Notes

1. On the term "massification" see Noël Carroll, "The Nature of Horror," *The Journal of Aesthetics and Art Criticism* 46 (1990): 50.
2. John Edgar Browning, "Survival Horrors, Survival Spaces: Tracing the Modern Zombie (Cine)Myth," *Horror Studies* 2 (2011): 41–59.
3. Ibid., 45.

4. Sylvia Bond, "Rocky Mountain Hell," *Pink Raygun*, February 26, 2008, accessed August 1, 2012, www.pinkraygun.com/2008/02/26/supernatural-jus-in-bello/.
5. Gregory A. Waller, *The Living and the Undead: From Stoker's Dracula to Romero's Dawn of the Dead* (Urbana: University of Illinois Press, 1986), 19.
6. Finishing this chapter would have been impossible without Galen Foresman's extraordinarily keen help on earlier drafts. His and series editor William Irwin's dedication is a credit to this anthology.

Part Three
EVIL BY DESIGN

Chapter 10

Dean Winchester and the *Supernatural* Problem of Evil

Daniel Haas

You would think that, for a person who spent most of his time fighting monsters and demons, it would be a foregone conclusion that God exists. I mean, if you've made deals with crossroad demons, matched wits against ancient demonic forces like Lilith and Crowley, then you know the bad guys of the major Western faiths exist. Surely, the ultimate good guy, God, must exist. Right?

And yet, even after years of demon-hunting, Dean, ever the skeptic, is still unconvinced. He's been to Heaven, Hell, Purgatory, and back, but he's still reluctant to acknowledge the existence of God. Is he just being stubborn? What more evidence for the existence of God could he possibly want? Or might Dean be rational in refusing to believe in God?

God's Not With Us, Not Anymore

So why doesn't Dean believe in the existence of God? Dean's lack of belief in God is first mentioned in the second season episode "Houses of the Holy." During this episode, the Winchesters are dealing with a group of people who claim that they've been told

Supernatural and Philosophy: Metaphysics and Monsters ... for Idjits, First Edition.
Edited by Galen A. Foresman.
© 2013 John Wiley & Sons, Inc. Published 2013 by John Wiley & Sons, Inc.

by angels to kill other people. Sam admits to Dean that he believes in God and that he often prays. Dean's response is, "There's no higher power, there's no God. There's just chaos and violence, random unpredictable evil, that comes outta nowhere, rips you to shreds."

Dean is likely more of an agnostic than an atheist. This takes center stage in the third season episode "Sin City," which begins with Sam learning of the mysterious deaths of the week. This time, "some guy blows his head off in a church and another goes postal in a hobby-shop before the cops take him out ..." Dean and Sam pose as insurance agents and travel to Elizabethville, Ohio, to investigate.

Upon arriving in town, they learn that the two deaths were not isolated incidents. A local hunter informs the brothers that demons have been possessing people for weeks. What should be a boarded-up old factory town has become a town full of people indulging in pleasure and sin. The brothers stop in at a local bar to do some research, and they meet a bartender named Casey who, unbeknownst to the brothers, is possessed by a demon. Dean hooks up with her and goes back to her place. Dean's date quickly turns into a fight, and Dean is trapped in the basement of Casey's home. Dean and Casey exchange verbal jabs which lead to Casey challenging Dean on theological issues:

DEAN: So demons take over. I thought that the meek shall inherit the earth.
CASEY: According to your bible. It's only a book Dean.
DEAN: Not everyone would agree.
CASEY: Because it's God's book. Do you believe in God Dean? I would be surprised if you did.
DEAN: I don't know. I would like to.
CASEY: Well I don't see how you and your god have done such a bang up job. War, genocide, it's only getting worse. I mean this past century you people racked up a body count that amazed even us.

Casey is alluding to one of the oldest and most resilient arguments against the existence of God, the problem of evil. This problem arises from an apparent conflict between the existence of evil and the attributes that Western theists attribute to God.

Theists traditionally hold the following four statements to be true:

1. God is all-powerful (Omnipotent).
2. God is all-knowing (Omniscient).
3. God is perfectly good (Omnibenevolent).
4. Evil exists.

But there seems to be a deep tension here. If God is perfectly good, it seems that God would not want evil to exist. And since God is all-knowing, God must know of every possibility for evil that exists in the world. Given that God is also all-powerful, surely God has the power to prevent any and all evil from occurring. So then why does the world contain so much evil? In fact, why is there any evil at all?

Casey poses a question that will haunt Dean long past this episode. If there's a God, why is there so much suffering and evil in the world? Surely a benevolent God would not preside over a world overrun by all this evil, all this suffering.

I Got to Believe That I Can Choose What I Do With My Unimportant Little Life

Casey's challenge to the existence of God is called the logical problem of evil by philosophers. Theists appear committed to a logically inconsistent set of claims, namely, that there exists an all-powerful, all-knowing, all-good God, and evil exists.

There are two options available for responding to a challenge like Casey's. First, Dean could give up one of the attributes of God. For example, Dean could claim that God is not really all-powerful and that is why God cannot eliminate evil. Or, maybe God doesn't actually know everything and so God simply doesn't know about some evils or doesn't know how to eliminate the evil that exists. It would even be possible for Dean to deny that God is perfectly good. If God isn't perfectly good, God might not desire to eliminate all evil. But making this move departs significantly from traditional conceptions of God, and that is something most Western theists would want to avoid.

You might say that the world of *Supernatural* is overpopulated by gods. The Winchesters have matched wits with Loki, Baal, and countless other gods from mythology. They even fought Paris Hilton, who guest-starred as a pagan god in "Fallen Idols." And none of these gods would fall victim to Casey's logical problem of evil. They are not all-powerful, all-knowing, and all-good, and so their existence is entirely consistent with the existence of evil. But the god that Casey mocks, the god that Dean has a difficult time believing in, is significantly different from these gods. It is the god of Western theism that is at issue here, and if that god exists, it is an all-good, all-powerful, and all-knowing god. So, Dean cannot simply say that God lacks one of these properties and that this is why there's evil in the world. If Casey's challenge is to be met, an alternative approach will have to be made.

The second way Dean could respond to an argument like Casey's would be to offer a theodicy, that is, an explanatory story for why an all-powerful, all-knowing, and all-good god would allow the existence of evil. Perhaps God has a very good reason for allowing evil to exist, and a good theodicy would explain God's reasoning.

The most common theodicy is to appeal to free will. Perhaps Dean could respond to Casey by saying that in order for free will to exist, God must allow for some evil. Specifically, God must allow humans to choose and cause evil to exist in the world. Why would this be the case? Because it is logically impossible to create free creatures and guarantee that they will never do evil. They must be able to choose between good and evil and, unfortunately, free creatures sometimes, perhaps even quite frequently, choose to do evil. But free will is such a great and amazing good, that it justifies the evil that God permits to exist.

Obviously, free will plays a central role in *Supernatural*. The entire fifth season focused on Sam and Dean having the freedom to choose whether to take part in a battle between the hosts of Heaven and Hell. In "Free to Be You and Me" during the fifth season, we learn that Sam is the chosen vessel for Lucifer to inhabit, while

Dean is the vessel for Michael. During the Apocalypse, these two angels are destined to possess the Winchesters and fight the final battle. Naturally, there's a catch. Both Sam and Dean have to freely choose to be used in this way.

If there's a God in the world of *Supernatural*, that God finds free will vitally important. So, perhaps we can understand God's commitment to the value of free will as a reasonable account for the existence of evil. It is a great good to allow creatures like humans to make their own choices, and one of the consequences of allowing for this kind of choice is that, on some occasions, evil will be freely chosen and produced. If this solution works, God could prevent evil, but to do so would be to eliminate free will.

So maybe Casey's challenge can be met. If Dean lacks faith in God merely because of Casey's argument, then it appears he doesn't have any good reason for not believing in God. But I think if we look at why Dean is so reluctant to believe in God, we'll see that his reasons are a bit different from those posed by the logical problem of evil.

A Theory With a Little Less Fairy Dust

As payment for a deal he made with a crossroad demon to save Sam's soul, Dean is dragged to Hell by hell-hounds at the end of the third season. Fortunately, Dean's stay in Hell isn't permanent, and the fourth season begins with Dean literally pulled from Hell by an angel. But even after this heavenly rescue, Dean stubbornly refuses to believe that God and angels exist. Upon meeting Castiel in "Lazarus Rising" and being told that angels really do exist, Dean responds to Castiel, "Get the Hell out of here! There's no such thing ..."

Dean is convinced that something else is going on, that there's a more reasonable explanation for how he escaped from Hell than that angels actually exist. In "Are You There God? It's Me, Dean Winchester," Dean discusses his angelic encounter with Sam:

DEAN: Don't you think that if angels were real, some hunter, somewhere, would've seen one, at some point, ever?

SAM: Yeah, you just did Dean.

> DEAN: I'm just trying to come up with a theory here. Work with me.
> SAM: Dean, we have a theory.
> DEAN: Yeah. One with a little less fairy dust on it, please.

Apparently the doubt that plagued Dean throughout the third season has gestated. Dean's now gone from skeptic to bona fide non-believer. Perhaps 40 years of being tortured in Hell will do that to a person. But Dean's got all the evidence he should need, right there. He can see and touch Castiel. Why isn't that enough?

One of the first things Dean wants to know from Castiel is *why* Castiel rescued him from Hell. Castiel's response is simple: "good things do happen." Obviously not satisfied, Dean retorts, "Not in my experience." Here we see Dean echoing Casey's earlier argument against the existence of God. The world is simply not a pleasant place. The world, as Dean sees it, is one of overwhelming evil. Good things rarely happen and are far overshadowed by an abundance of tragedy and suffering. Now Dean is expected to believe not only that there are angels and a God, but that they're looking out for him? That's too much for him. Maybe demons and vampires exist. But a loving God and his servants that are watching over Dean and Sam? Not likely.

Just Random Horrible Evil

Dean's problem of evil is slightly different from the version we considered earlier. Casey's problem of evil focused on an apparent logical inconsistency between believing in a God that is all-powerful, all-knowing, and all-good, while at the same time believing that evil exists. But Dean's concern isn't really about logical consistency. He has a different and perhaps deeper concern. In "Are You There God? It's Me, Dean Winchester," Dean voices his reluctance to believe in God to Bobby and Sam:

> DEAN: See this is why I can't get behind God. If he doesn't exist, fine. Bad crap happens to good people. That's how it is. There's no rhyme or reason, just random horrible evil, I get it. I can roll with that. But if he is out there, what's wrong

> with him? Where the Hell is he while all these decent
> people are getting torn to shreds? How does he live with
> himself? You know, why doesn't he help?
>
> BOBBY: I ain't touching this one with a ten foot pole.

Dean is presenting an argument known as the *evidential problem of evil*. He is not claiming that the attributes commonly associated with God are inconsistent with the existence of evil, as they were in the *logical problem of evil* discussed earlier. Rather, Dean's claim is that the *severity* and *amount* of evil present in the world is inconsistent with the traditional God of theists (again, an all-powerful, all-knowing, and all-good God).

Dean is not concerned that the existence of evil is simply inconsistent with God. Rather, Dean is concerned that God is very *unlikely* to exist in a world that contains the kinds of extreme and apparently pointless suffering that Dean encounters on a day-to-day basis. Not the least of which are the pointless tragic deaths from demons spilling forth from the gates of Hell and all those who die from more common monsters like ghosts and werewolves.

And these are just the supernatural causes of suffering. Never mind all the people who suffer from the typical senseless tragedies like disease, natural disasters, famine, and starvation. Bad things happen to good people all of the time. If there is no higher power, no higher purpose to it all, then the world's merely a dangerous, messy place, and Dean can handle that. He can carry on. He can carve out the best life he can and try to minimize some of the senseless tragedy in the process. But if there's a God, that whole picture changes.

If there's a God, then the degree of evil in the world should be much less severe than what Dean's experienced. An all-powerful, all-knowing, and all-good God could have prevented much of the tragedy in the world without suffering the loss of any greater good. Perhaps some evils are justified by the existence of great goods like free will, but certainly not *all* the evils Dean is concerned with, like creatures whose sole purpose is to cause suffering. For example, by allowing for the existence of the rakshasa from "Everybody Love a Clown," a monster devoted to eating human flesh, God does not promote some greater good. These monsters simply torture and kill innocent people. What's more disturbing, the God that Dean is being asked to believe in is ultimately responsible for creating these monsters.

Take the rugaru as another example. It is a pitiful creature. The rugaru begins its life as a human, but eventually, it transforms into a flesh-eating monster, primarily human flesh at that. During the rugaru's life as a human, it develops an insatiable hunger. In "Metamorphosis," the Winchesters tracked a poor middle-aged man, whose rugaru nature had just activated. He found himself eating everything he could get his hands on in a desperate attempt to satisfy his hunger. But his hunger grew throughout the episode until he found himself hungrily eying his wife. Now, obviously, if God exists in the world of *Supernatural*, God not only allows the pathetic, cursed rugaru to degenerate into a truly tragic beast of mindless hunger and carnage, but God ultimately created the rugaru. God created a creature that would live a tortured life, loving and caring for a spouse, even as it was compelled to eat that spouse alive. What possible theodicy would justify God's work here?

Dean is convinced that his world makes sense only if there's no God. There's loads of evil out there, but ultimately, that's the way things are. There's no higher purpose for all this suffering, and there's no God with a plan who's intentionally letting all this happen. The moment God is introduced into this picture, you have an all-powerful, all-knowing being that refuses to lift a finger to help, and this very same God is ultimately the source of all this suffering. Who could respect or worship a God like that?

Dean says it best when he voices his skepticism about God to Castiel. In that bit of dialogue, he lets Castiel know what he thinks of angels and gods that are willing to allow the world's many evils to persist.

DEAN: I thought angels were supposed to be guardians, fluffy wings, halos, you know, Michael Landon, not dicks.
CASTIEL: Read the Bible. Angels are warriors of God. I'm a soldier.
DEAN: Yeah, why didn't you fight?

CASTIEL: I'm not here to perch on your shoulder. We had larger concerns.

DEAN: Concerns? There are people getting torn to shreds down here. And by the way, while all this is going on, where the Hell is your boss, huh, if there is a God.

CASTIEL: There's a God.

DEAN: I'm not convinced. 'Cause if there's a God, what the Hell is he waiting for? Huh? Genocide? Monsters roaming the earth? The fricken Apocalypse? At what point does he lift a damn finger and help the poor bastards that are stuck down here?

CASTIEL: The Lord works ...

DEAN: If you say "mysterious ways," so help me, I will kick your ass.

No, He's Not on Any Flatbread

What's interesting about Dean's struggle with the existence of God is that it's never fully resolved. After eight seasons, he has yet to come to terms with God, or even to acknowledge that God must exist, even if it's a God that he's not all that fond of. And no one, not Sam, Bobby, or Castiel provides Dean with a good enough reason to think that God exists given the obvious presence of apparently senseless evil in the world. Hell, Dean's even been to Heaven, and he still doesn't believe.

Can Dean's challenge be met? Is there anything to be said in God's defense? One way the theist could try to satisfy Dean would be to argue that many of the things Dean has identified as evil are not really evils. For example, when a rakshasa kills a human to eat its flesh, we shouldn't consider this evil. We are simply looking at the natural order of things, and the human race is merely another animal in the food chain. Lions feed on gazelles. Humans feed on all sorts of animals, and all of this is simply the natural order of things. The lion must eat the gazelle to survive, and throughout much of human history humans have needed to eat other animals to survive. Likewise, when the rakshasa, the vampires, and the leviathan of *Supernatural* consume human flesh or blood, they are simply doing what they need to in order to survive.

On this view, humans are not significantly different than the animals we eat. If there's any difference, it is that our mental faculties allow us to question our behavior. Unlike the lions that feed on gazelles, we are able to ask, "why?" And this leads many of us to question our meat-eating behavior, not because we think we're engaging in evil, but because we have sophisticated enough mental faculties to recognize that when another creature dies at our hands, we should try to minimize the amount of suffering it experiences ..." Many of the monsters of *Supernatural* are capable of the same empathy and concern for those they kill. For example, while the leviathans of Season 7 do attempt to take over the Earth, they did so primarily to ensure an ample supply of food-stock. Recognizing that killing humans for food causes suffering, Dick Roman, leader of the leviathans, ensures that the domestication of humans is done in a humane way. Roman Enterprises actually attempts to drug humans in such a way that they are passive and unafraid. Humans are fed food that they love and are allowed to laze about for days on end. The leviathans even took it upon themselves to cure cancer and create food sources that would minimize human starvation worldwide.

The leviathans were not really evil. They were simply creatures whose primary food-source happened to be humans. It was just part of the natural order. Now, the theist could point to this idea that humans are merely animals, and as animals we are no more special or privileged than any other creature that inhabits Earth, Heaven, Purgatory, or Hell. It is simply part of the natural order that things are this way. And when Dean defiantly challenges God, demanding that God intervene on behalf of humanity to stop the monsters, demons, leviathans, and other creatures that come in conflict with the human race, God could reply:

> Why? What makes you, so special? You're no better or worse than the delicious cow you had for lunch. Like it or not, you're a tasty meal for many creatures out there.

Probably no theodicy would satisfy Dean given the life he's lived, but there are a couple reasons Dean might legitimately be skeptical about this natural-order theodicy. First, if there is a God, then God is the ultimate creator of everything, both natural and supernatural. God, by creating the universe, set things in motion, including the natural order of things. So, any flaws in the natural order are on God's shoulders. If there are *unnecessary* evils in the world, those speak against God's perfect goodness, his power, his knowledge, or his competence. Why didn't God make a world where creatures don't eat each other? Dean can fairly point out that appealing to the natural order is a cop-out. God set the rules of the game, and if those rules promote horrendous suffering, why didn't an all-powerful, all-knowing, and all-good God do better? Or maybe, as Dean concludes, the existence of all this suffering just goes to show that it's highly unlikely that this creator God exists, at least not the omni-perfect God of Western theism.

Second, note that many of the creatures in *Supernatural* fully recognize that killing other creatures to survive inflicts intense anguish and suffering on their victims. This is true of humans, rugaru, leviathan, and many of the other denizens of the *Supernatural* universe. While it is a relatively recent phenomenon in human history to concern ourselves with the suffering of the creatures we eat, it is something we're quickly becoming concerned with as we move into the twenty-first century. We are aware that if we don't take care to treat our food-stock with the utmost respect they'll suffer pointlessly at our hands. Perhaps the natural order is cruel, but we don't need to be.

Therefore, even if there was some reason why the natural order was initially brutal, filled with pointless suffering for all sorts of creatures, both humans and leviathans are aware that this suffering can be minimized. Our mental faculties are limited compared to God, so, again, the ball is thrown back into God's court. If we can see how we can do better with the suffering of animals by giving them happy lives and painless deaths, then surely God could have anticipated this. God could have designed things differently, which means God did a bad job when he created the universe.

At this point, someone might ask, "Who are we to judge God?" Even God has apparently said as much in the Book of Job to the frustrated pleas of a man who has seen the world like Dean. There

God says, "Who is this that darkens counsel by words without knowledge?" (38:2).

Certainly, answering a question with another question isn't going to satisfy Dean. Keep in mind that traditionally God is thought to be worthy of worship not merely because God is an all-powerful thing from which we should cower in fear. Rather, God is an omnibenevolent being and worthy of worship precisely because of that perfect goodness. The challenge of Dean and Job isn't the narcissistic plea of a childish species over-stepping its bounds, daring to question God. Instead, the challenge is that if flawed creatures like humans and leviathans can do better, then surely God can, and if God chooses not to, then God's either unable to or God is unwilling to. In either case, this is not the God of Western theism.

Dean has little patience for demons, monsters, angels, and gods that aren't willing to use their powers to make the world a better place. As far as Dean is concerned, if you act like a monster, you're a monster, and it really doesn't matter how powerful you are or what they call you in holy books. When Castiel claimed the powers of Heaven as his own, essentially becoming a god, Dean didn't bow down and worship Castiel. Rather, Dean tried to reason with his former friend, and when that failed, Dean went searching for a way to destroy him. Likewise, a theodicy that appeals to the natural order of things isn't going to satisfy Dean, it's only going to make him hunt down the monster that created the natural order.

Please Give Me a Chance …

There's a further theodicy that Dean hasn't considered. Perhaps the reason God doesn't intervene in this world isn't because God doesn't exist or doesn't care or isn't able. Maybe the reason God doesn't intervene in this world to minimize the suffering of the human race and everyone else in *Supernatural* is because the world isn't supposed to be a perfect place. Maybe all this suffering serves a purpose.

Perhaps our world is intended as a proving ground, a place for forging souls. Maybe it is a greater good to create a universe in which free but imperfect creatures rise above their fragilities and cultivate virtuous characters, souls worthy of salvation and communion with God. While it might be a great thing if God created a world full of perfectly virtuous creatures, wouldn't it be even more amazing if God created a world where imperfect creatures grew through their choices and trials to become virtuous creatures? Isn't there something admirable about the self-made hero who overcomes a life of adversity, something that would be lost if the hero was simply born into a life of comfort? Philosopher John Hick (1922–2012) proposes this very theodicy as a solution to the evidential problem of evil in "An Irenaean Theodicy."[1]

The universe of *Supernatural* lends itself to Hick's soul-making theodicy. Retribution and reward are undeniably present. Whether one is pulled down to Hell by hell-hounds after dealing with a crossroads demon or ascending to Heaven after living a pious life, the idea that our deeds in this world weigh positively or negatively on our soul is a common theme in the show.

So, maybe soul-making is the reason God doesn't intervene on Dean's behalf. Maybe allowing for evil creates opportunities for humans to cultivate more perfect souls, to become worthy of Heaven and eternal salvation. But if soul-making really is a good thing, it doesn't justify all evils. It only justifies the amount of evil and suffering that would be necessary for humans to have opportunities to cultivate Heaven-worthy souls. Any evil and suffering above and beyond that simply isn't justified in this theodicy. But the *Supernatural* universe seems to have much more suffering and evil than this minimal amount. It's a universe bursting at the seams with adversity and strife.

Consider the rugaru, again. It is a creature with a very important life choice, a truly soul-making choice. If a rugaru never consumes human flesh, then it will never complete its descent into absolute monstrosity. It will simply live out its life suffering from a nearly irresistible urge to consume human flesh. It will live a life of agony, but perhaps overcoming and resisting this temptation is a way for the rugaru to cultivate a Heaven-worthy soul.

Does this seem like a fair soul-making challenge? The deck is stacked pretty severely against this poor creature. I suspect that the vast majority of rugaru fail at this challenge. If the plight of the rugaru is really an opportunity for piety in disguise, it sure seems like an unfair challenge. Couldn't an all-knowing, all-perfect, and all-powerful God come up with a fair challenge? One where the deck wasn't so strongly stacked against the poor rugaru? One that didn't result in so much suffering for innocent bystanders if the rugaru failed?

Likewise, couldn't the great heroism, compassion, and charity cultivated in the Winchesters from a lifetime of fighting monsters and demons be accomplished in a far less bloody way? Couldn't an all-powerful god create a universe where there were ample opportunities to help the elderly across the street? Or what about a world where there are abundant opportunities to show compassion by removing splinters from the paws of puppies? Does the moral growth and soul-making of Sam and Dean really require that an apocalypse be averted every year?

Unfortunately, the soul-making defense doesn't appear to be enough to solve the problem for Dean. While it seems true that an all-powerful, all-good, all-knowing God would have the power to create a universe with soul-growth, containing significantly less evil and suffering than the universe of *Supernatural*, that's just not Dean's world. Thus, it's reasonable for him to question the very existence of God.

Where does this leave us? Is this really the best of all possible worlds? Is this really as good as it gets? Or, are we like Dean, trapped in a world filled with excess pain, suffering, and evil? And if our world's more like Dean's, perhaps that leaves us asking the same question that's plagued Dean for years. Are you there, God?[2]

Notes

1. John H. Hick, "An Irenaean Theodicy," in Stephen T. Davis ed., *Encountering Evil: Live Options in Theodicy* (Atlanta: John Knox Press, 1981), 39–68.
2. *Supernatural* is ultimately about the bond between two brothers, and this one has to be for Matthew Haas.

Chapter 11

Angels and Atheists

Fredrick Curry

CASTIEL: ... I still serve God.

URIEL: You haven't even met the man. There is no will. No
            wrath. No God.

"On the Head of a Pin"

We often lament our limited nature as human beings. *Supernatural* is certainly no stranger to this theme and often contrasts the many weaknesses of man to the awesome power of angels, demons, and otherworldly creatures. Mankind is always out-muscled in its dealings with supernatural powerhouses, but the dramatic differences are quickly narrowed as soon as Sam and Dean call good ol' Bobby Singer. Bobby always has the right information at just the right time. He gives the Winchester boys the perspective they need to handle everything from gods to ghosts to brotherly love.

Most of the time, however, even Bobby's understanding of the world around us pales in comparison to that of angels and demons. I don't know if they just have a better education system in Heaven and Hell, but for whatever reason, they just seem to know more about the way the universe works than any mortal person on Earth. You and I struggle with difficult philosophical questions like: What is the meaning of life? Are there such things as miracles? What happens when we die? Does God exist? So it's easy to suppose that if

Supernatural and Philosophy: Metaphysics and Monsters ... for Idjits, First Edition.
Edited by Galen A. Foresman.
© 2013 John Wiley & Sons, Inc. Published 2013 by John Wiley & Sons, Inc.

we just shared in such a "higher" perspective, like that of angels and demons, we would know the answer to many of life's big questions. But I think that even if beings such as angels existed, they would not necessarily be in a better position to answer some of life's more philosophical mysteries. Like Uriel in the quote above from "On the Head of a Pin," angels on *Supernatural* can reasonably be atheists.

Some angels claim to have actually seen God and conversed with him, like Lucifer, Michael, and Gabriel. But the vast majority of angels in Heaven must take it on faith that God exists. In a particularly moving scene from the episode "Heaven and Hell," Dean questions Anna, the angel who fell from grace to live on Earth, as to why she would leave the heavenly host:

ANNA: Dean, do you know how many angels have actually seen God? Seen his face?
DEAN: All of you?
ANNA: Four angels. Four. And I'm not one of them.
DEAN: That's it? Well, then how do you even know that there is a God?
ANNA: We have to take it on faith … which we're killed if we don't have.
DEAN: Huh.

For the sake of simplicity, let's focus on whether angels like Anna and Cas should believe God exists. After all, they can't exactly take Lucifer at his word, and the show doesn't portray his brothers as any more trustworthy. Let's not forget, Gabriel is the "Trickster."

Good God Y'all

Before arguing that angels can reasonably be atheists, we should first get clear about what "God" we're talking about. After all, there have clearly been "gods" at work in the series. Sam and Dean have met Kali, Zao Shen, Veritas, Osiris, Chronos, Plutus, Vili, Odin, Ganesh, Baldur, Leshii, and others, and even dispatched a good portion of them. So, it isn't just *any* god that we're talking about. No, the type of god being doubted fits the profile of the Judeo-Christian God, to whom the following six properties are commonly attributed:

1. Omnipotence (all powerful/can do anything)
2. Omniscience (all knowing/knows everything)
3. Omnibenevolence (all good/always does good/always is good)
4. Original creator of everything in the universe
5. Conscious, personal being
6. Eternal[1]

One of these properties deserves some extra attention before proceeding. "Omnipotence" can be problematic. Taken in the *hard sense* it would literally mean that God could do anything. But suppose that a more philosophically inclined Dean were to ask the following question: Could God create a woman so hot that even God couldn't resist her?

There are really only two possible answers to the question— "Yes" or "No." If the answer for us is "Yes, God could," then we're admitting that there is something that God cannot do— resist the hot woman he created. In this case, we're saying God *can* make her, but he *can't* resist her. If, on the other hand, we say "No, God could *not* create such a woman," then there is very clearly something God can't do. Only this time, he can't even create the hot woman.

Because of this problem "omnipotence" is often taken in a *softer sense* to mean, "Can do anything that is logically possible." Under this interpretation, what we might call *Dean's Hot Woman Objection* to God's existence evaporates, since the challenge to create such a woman involves a logical impossibility. Similar logical impossibilities occur when we ask whether God could create a square circle, a Euclidean triangle with internal angles that sum to more than 180 degrees, or an invisible *black* Impala. The *softer sense* of "omnipotence" says that it is no real limitation on God's power to say that he cannot create such silly things, since all logical impossibilities are really just "nonsense." You may use real words to ask about an invisible black Impala or a square circle, but they are not expressing any meaningful concept. You may as well be asking, "Could God blahblahblahblahblah?" And if the question itself is nonsense, then it isn't fair to say that God can't do it. After all, we don't even know what we're talking about when we say "square circle" or "invisible, black Impala."

Since our point will be even more dramatic if every advantage is given to our opponents, we'll investigate whether or not it is reasonable for angels to doubt God's existence in the *softer sense* of the word "omnipotent." And while I hate to deny Dean his hot woman, this does avoid the immediate game-ender *Dean's Hot Woman Objection*.

Clap Your Hands if You Believe

DEAN: There's no higher power; there's no God. I mean, there's just chaos, and violence, and random unpredictable evil that comes out of nowhere and rips you to shreds. You want me to believe in this stuff? I'm going to need to see some hard proof. You got any?

"Houses of the Holy"

Historically, there have been many attempted proofs of God's existence. Curiously, some of these proofs contradict one another. For example, Tertullian (160–225) argued that one should believe in God partly because belief in God is absurd, but the *ontological argument* says that disbelief in God is absurd. Of course, not all arguments for the existence of God have been considered equally strong, which is why so many of them are not discussed anymore.

Fortunately, it should be enough to show that angels can reasonably be atheists by showing two things. First, the best arguments in favor of the existence of God are no better if Anna and Cas think about them, and second, that these angels are also in no better position than we are to deny what is perhaps the strongest argument *against* the existence of God. In other words, we'll see that Anna and Cas have no better arguments in favor of God than we do, and that they also don't have any better way to defend against arguments that are intended to prove there is no God.

In the Beginning ...

The cosmological argument for the existence of God begins with a couple of observations about the universe. The first is pretty obvious—"things exist." The second is that everything that exists was caused to exist as it is. This is fairly obvious to most people too, but our belief in this second observation comes to us through many, many experiences that we have with the world around us. For example, Dean's Impala exists as it does as a result of prior causes. Dents on the hood could have been caused when a demon threw itself on the hood last week. Its current location was probably caused by Sam or Dean driving it to that location. The burger wrappers in the back seat were caused by Dean's late-night junk-food cravings. The point is, whatever aspect of the car we might consider, it seems to have been caused to be in that state by something that occurred prior in time. Chuck Shurley toys with this idea in the first few lines of "Swan Song":

> Three days later, another car rolled off that same line. No one gave two craps about her. But they should have, because this 1967 Chevrolet Impala would turn out to be the most important car—no, the most important *object*—in pretty much the whole universe.

Had Chuck wanted to, he could have stretched this chain of events even further back to what caused the engineers to design the vehicle in the way that they did. But our search for earlier causation doesn't have to end there. We could go on to consider what caused the designers to become engineers, and what caused their parents to have children in the first place, and what caused their grandparents to have children when they did, and so forth, backward in time indefinitely.

Of course, Chuck wouldn't write a story like this, because these sorts of causes seem to go on backward without end. Ultimately, this never gives us an explanation for why things are as they are now. The problem isn't just that each explanation needs another explanation, because we know that some explanations are really very interesting. The problem with a story like this is that each explanation gives basically the same repetitive kind of explanation. Each step of the explanation demands a new explanation of exactly the same sort that we were trying to resolve in the first place, and what is worse, this seems to go backward in terms of causation forever. This problem is known as an *infinite regress*.

Why is an infinite regress a problem? If Chuck really had to start "Swan Song" at the beginning, where would he begin? If causes can be traced back forever, then there is never an actual beginning or starting point for the causal process. If, for example, there are an infinite number of things that had to occur to get the Impala in the right place at the end of "Swan Song," and all these things have to take some amount of time, then an infinite amount of time is necessary to save the world from the Apocalypse with the help of the Impala. But it is impossible to cross over an infinite amount of time, and so averting the Apocalypse would be impossible. In fact, according to this argument, anything that occurs with an infinite regress of prior causes is impossible.

Since we ended up with this regress because of the two observations we made about the universe, there must be something wrong with one of our original observations. It's impossible to doubt the first one, things exist (just try it!). Therefore, there must be some exception to our second observation, which stated that all things that exist must have been caused to exist in that way. What could an exception to this observation be? It would have to be some sort of cause that was itself uncaused. This *uncaused cause* or *first cause* was identified as God by the famous philosopher and theologian St. Thomas Aquinas (c. 1225–1274).

This has historically been an exceptionally influential argument for the existence of God, and, indeed, it is usually behind the first criticism leveled against any atheist brave enough to express her views publicly. "Well then," the theistic critic demands, "if you don't believe in God, how do you think we got here?" The implication is that God is needed to kick things off—to push over the first domino in the cosmic chain of causal events.

There are, however, numerous historical criticisms of the cosmological argument. For example, in quantum physics there are events that are indeed truly uncaused. Subatomic particles literally blink into existence from nothing and blink out again. Many physicists, including Stephen Hawking, suggest that the entire universe was at one point much smaller than a proton, and given such quantum laws, it is quite possible that the universe popped into being from nothing. This would have occurred with no violation of the current laws of physics and just prior to the Big Bang. In which case, the universe would exist without God kicking it all off.

Another problem arises for the argument if we consider whether the first cause must be God. At best, the argument proves that there must be some uncaused cause. But recalling the six properties of God, we can see that a mere "uncaused cause" falls far short of being the God we described. This uncaused cause, whatever it is, need not be conscious, all-powerful, all-knowing, omnibenevolent, omniscient, or eternal. Thus, the cosmological argument we've been discussing fails to prove that God exists.

Importantly, it is a mistake to think that this argument shows that it is even *reasonable* to believe in such a God. In other words, the argument taken alone gives us no additional evidence for God's existence. The argument *only* gives us reason to suppose an initial cause, not an omniscient, omnibenevolent, omnipotent, personal, conscious, eternal one. We have no more reason to suppose the existence of God after accepting the argument than we did without it.

Notice that introducing supernatural beings into this scenario does nothing to make the argument better. Even if you yourself were an angel like Cas or Anna, you would have no new information that would strengthen this argument. You might say, "Well, the existence of supernatural beings shows that other kinds of supernatural beings, like God, *could* exist." But remember that the argument being considered is whether or not God, a very *specific* supernatural being, exists. At most, an angel could learn from this argument that there was an uncaused cause, and from that some supernatural beings emerged. But none of those supernatural beings need to be God. The argument fails to deliver, for humans or angels.

Wishful Thinking

The demise of the cosmological argument doesn't mean all hope is lost. We might argue that angels are at least in a better position than human beings to know whether or not living things were designed by a God. The *argument from design* was given by Thomas Aquinas and others but it was popularized and presented in great detail by William Paley (1743–1805). In brief, the argument goes something like this: If we were to stumble upon some sort of device out in the middle of a barren natural landscape, for example, a '67 Impala in the middle of the desert, we could determine that the Impala must have had a designer. Paley argues that the rocks, the sand, and so forth might have been there forever as far as we know, but there is something special about a vehicle that makes it different than these other things.

It isn't just that the Impala is shiny or smooth. It isn't the fact that we all already know an automobile when we see it. The following features distinguish the Impala from the rocks and sand around it:

- The entire thing seems to have a function.
- Its parts each seem to have functions.
- The materials of the parts seem well suited for their apparent functions.
- The parts are interrelated and interact together to serve other functions.

If we look at living things, we notice these same features. For example, the organs of a living creature interrelate and perform specific functions like the motor and transmission of an Impala. Organs are made out of materials well suited for their function, and they are all organized in such a way that allows them to fulfill their function. For example, if the tendons and bones in the hand were crossed or attached in different places, grip and dexterity would be severely compromised. Therefore, just as we can tell that the Impala has a designer, we can also conclude that living things have a designer. At the end of the day, most living things are far more complex than an Impala, so we must conclude that God is the designer of living things.

A potential problem with this argument was recognized by Paley himself. If there were a principle of nature which could explain how an Impala might form through natural physical laws, the mystery of the finding the Impala in the desert would be solved without relying on a designer. The Impala could just occur naturally. Paley's response at the time was that we know of no such laws. What natural law makes Impalas? Of course, the problem for Paley was that his work *Natural Theology* was published in 1802, more than 50 years before Charles Darwin published *The Origin of Species* in 1859. Therein, Darwin explains how the principle of natural selection is a natural process that accounts for the functionality of organs and tissue in very complicated living things without assuming a designer created them, which, of course, undermines the design argument.

What about supernatural beings like angels? Does the argument from design fare any better when we assume they exist? According to "The Man Who Would Be King," the existence of angels coincides with the process of natural selection. Castiel says:

> You know, I've … I've been here for a very long time. And I remember many things. *(an ocean is shown)* I remember being at a shoreline, watching a little grey fish heave itself up on the beach and an older brother saying, "Don't step on that fish Castiel. Big plans for that fish."

Two other possible lines of argument might be taken from this. Either evolution itself is the *method* of design, or angels know that they themselves were not the products of evolution. In either case, God must exist as the designer of evolution or as the designer of angels. While we mere mortals wouldn't have access to this information, it would still be reasonable for angels to believe in God.

Unfortunately for this line of argument, there are still objections to be made. For example, evolution as a method of design implies that the designer isn't fully competent to engineer the end result without the help of evolution. Why would an omnipotent God need help? Also, evolution is an incredibly *inefficient* way to engineer anything. Evolution in the form of natural and artificial selection is indeed a useful engineering tool, but it is only useful in the same way that all trial and error approaches are useful. The problem, of course, is that an omniscient God wouldn't need trial and error as an engineering tool. An all-knowing God would know how to create without the use of natural selection. Therefore, if we think evolution was the method of design, then that is all the more reason to believe that an omnipotent and omniscient God does *not* exist.

But what about the second line of argument? What if angels themselves know that they didn't evolve? They are, after all, supernatural, so maybe they aren't biological organisms at all. Unfortunately, that simply puts them in the same position human beings were in before Darwin's theory of natural selection. They simply do not *yet* know a way to explain their functionality, but someday they may. They cannot rationally conclude from their lack of understanding that God designed them. To reason like this would be to commit a common fallacy known as an *appeal to ignorance.*

But is God at least a *reasonable* explanation from the point of view angels? No, because angels have endless examples of natural laws explaining complex behaviors and creations in the universe that don't require God. These include the formation of planets, the orbits of planets, the growth of biological organisms, on through the origin of individual species. The principle of parsimony is the principle that, all other things being equal, the simplest solution is most likely the correct one. And in this case, it would suggest to angels that there is an explanation of this sort waiting to be discovered. Why would they be an exception?

Are You There, God? It's Me, Dean Winchester

We've now considered the two most prevalent arguments for the existence of God from the perspective of angels, and it turns out that they have no more reason to believe in God than we do. What remains to consider is whether or not angels are better off answering one of the strongest arguments *against* the existence of God, aptly named "the argument from evil."

The argument from evil proceeds by highlighting an apparent conflict in God's attributes when we contrast them with how terrible things can be here on Earth. Imagine an omnipotent, omniscient, and omnibenevolent God. Not only would that God be able to eliminate all evil with literally no effort, but that God would know about all the evil that exists in the world today. Furthermore, that God would be so good that it wouldn't willingly allow all that evil to exist. So if the God we're imagining really exists, then what's with all the evil in the world? The only reasonable thing to conclude is that our imagined God doesn't exist in actuality.

The first thing to notice is that this only argues against the existence of a particular *kind* of God. It wouldn't, for example, argue against the existence of a God like Zeus, Odin, or some other deity that was not meant to be all good, all knowing, or all powerful. Actually, if we remove any of the three traits of God mentioned above, the argument from evil fails. If God is all knowing and all good, but *not* all powerful, then evil might exist simply because God is not powerful enough to do away with it. If God is all powerful and all good, but *not* all knowing, then evil might still exist because God doesn't know about some of it. Finally, if God is all powerful and all knowing, but *not* all good, then God could decide to allow some evil to exist because He's not fully good Himself. As it stands, however, combining the three components of omnipotence, omniscience, and omnibenevolence results in a God that is incompatible with the existence of evil.

One way to object to this argument is to suggest that there isn't evil in the world. Of course, making this objection opens you up to a lot of obvious criticisms. Dean, for example, might point to all the instances of his own suffering, Sam's suffering, and the suffering of many others. In the real world we might point to floods, famine, childhood cancer, genetic disorders, plagues, pestilence, and so on. To deny that evil exists when so many people experience it needlessly everyday would be a stretch. On the other hand, if it is granted that evil does exist, then it seems to contradict the conclusion that God exists.

The argument from evil has been such a powerful and long-standing argument against the existence of God that there is even a special name for arguments that try to reconcile the existence of evil with the existence God. These arguments are called "theodicies." We will look at a couple of the strongest to show that they work no better for angels than for humans. As a result, angels can't wield them in their defense.

Perhaps the most common theodicy is the claim that evil is the result of human free will. According to this claim, free will is so good that it outweighs the evil produced by it. Ultimately, God had a choice between giving humans free will and eliminating all evil. Eliminating all evil would mean eliminating free will, and eliminating free will would reduce the total good in the world. Being all good, God chose the greater good of keeping free will over the lesser good of eliminating the evil it produces. As the free will theodicy goes, evil exists not because God directly produced it, but only because he gave human beings free will and *they* produced evil. Therefore, God is still omniscient, omnipotent, omnibenevolent, *and* there is evil in the world, But that's our stupid fault!

There are at least two major problems with this line of reasoning. For starters, why didn't God create human beings with free will who made better choices? After all, human beings commit evil acts, because they are *tempted* to do so. Why not make the world with fewer temptations? Or at least make humans in such a way that they are only slightly tempted by evil, but their goodness always prevails. There is nothing contradictory about God creating humans and the universe we interact with such that we could choose evil if we really wanted to but we are never quite pushed to the point of doing so.

More problematic for this theodicy is the existence of *natural evils*. If we accept the free will theodicy, it explains why evils such as slavery, wars, murder, and so forth exist. But how does it explain smallpox? How does it explain droughts and famine? How does it explain hookworms, malaria, cancer, muscular dystrophy, dysentery, tornadoes, and that one annoying cricket you can never seem to get out of your kitchen? At best, free choice can explain the suffering that results from *human-produced evils*, not the blows mankind suffers at the hands of nature itself.

Again, having angelic knowledge seems to be of no help. What additional information could Cas or Anna supply that would resolve the issue? It isn't as though they have deeper insight into human psychology, able to give us more accurate information about human motivations. This is made abundantly clear in "Caged Heat" when Cas remarks, "If the pizza man truly loves this baby-sitter, why does he keep slapping her rear? Perhaps she's done something wrong." But perhaps these characters are so smart and so powerful that they can see long-term consequences of events. Perhaps they can see how an evil now turns out to produce a greater good later. For example, Sam and Dean's mother is killed by the yellow-eyed demon, which is bad, but that turns out to produce a weightier good later by furthering the monster-slaying Winchester legacy. Unfortunately, we would have to presume that *all* such evils are outweighed by greater future goods, which seems unlikely. Thus, Anna and Cas are left in the same position as their human counterparts.

In fact, even if *all* evils produced a greater good, that's still not enough to show that God is all good. Couldn't God have made the same goods or the same amount of good *without* producing the evils along the way? God is all powerful, after all. Even if one supposes that in just one case just *some* suffering is unnecessary, that proves that God cannot be all good while at the same time being all powerful and all knowing. Are we honestly to believe that a two-year-old dying of dehydration in a foreign land is necessary for us to have the best possible world? If God stopped just one of those deaths, would the world suddenly be worse off?

Out With the Old

So where does this leave the angels? It leaves them pretty much in the same position we're in. They are more powerful than we are, for certain; they live longer; they're smarter; and they have powers we can't explain. Nevertheless, it is no more reasonable for them to conclude that God exists than it would be for us. Therefore, as we watch and enjoy Eric Kripke's storytelling in *Supernatural*, it would serve us well to remember that *all* the supernatural creatures in the series are works of fiction—not just the ones that go bump in the night. And, ironically, we atheists can finally say we are on the side of the angels.

Note

1. Technically, Death says that he will eventually reap God in "Two Minutes to Midnight," but, for the sake of argument, let us call this close enough to "eternal" for our purposes.

Chapter 12

Oh God, You Devil

Danilo Chaib

God's character remains one of the big mysteries in *Supernatural*. Unlike other characters, God never really makes a physical appearance, so it's difficult to figure out what he or she is like.[1] We certainly see God's impact on the world, and occasionally, we're told he has miraculously interceded on behalf of the Winchesters or Castiel. We've seen, for example, God rescue Sam and Dean from the release of Lucifer from his Cage, and in "Dark Side of the Moon," the angel Joshua relays a clear but gentle command from God to "Back off."

Of course, God gets quite a bit of bad press by allowing evil to exist in the world, and mankind's unfettered ability to think freely leads Dean to wonder whether, "he's just going to sit back and watch the world burn ... just another dead-beat dad with a bunch of excuses."[2] But Dean was also skeptical of angels, even after Castiel appeared to him, so we should take his general pessimism for what it's worth, saying more about his personality than the evidence around him.

So what evidence could Dean look to for understanding God's character? Is there enough good in the world to say that on the whole he cares about his creation or loves the being in it? And if he does, what do we make of Hell? Would he support Sam and Dean's plan to close its gates forever?

Supernatural and Philosophy: Metaphysics and Monsters ... for Idjits, First Edition.
Edited by Galen A. Foresman.
© 2013 John Wiley & Sons, Inc. Published 2013 by John Wiley & Sons, Inc.

Ruby's Lesson

In his *Meditations*, the philosopher René Descartes (1596–1650) reasons, "For what is more self-evident than the fact that the Supreme Being exists, or that God, to whose essence alone existence belongs, exists?"[3] Descartes' point is that God's very essence is to be the Supreme Being. "Supreme," is, of course, the important word. We're not talking about the pagan gods that sometimes show up on *Supernatural*; we're talking about the God of Judaism, Christianity, and Islam. In fact, this notion of being *supreme* is probably what leads Castiel to think he's God when he's filled with all the souls from Purgatory. Cas was probably thinking, "I'm now the Supreme Being, so I must be God."

In addition to a supreme being, Descartes believed in the possibility of demons. He even believed in the possibility of a demon who is supremely powerful, cunning, and spends all its time and energy deceiving human beings.[4] Think of Ruby, the beautiful female demon who was supposed to be Sam's ally against Lilith but who was actually using him as the key to releasing Lucifer from Hell. Ruby deceives Sam, but Dean is a tougher nut to crack, since he's ever skeptical of her good intentions. Consider this particularly revealing bit of dialogue from "Malleus Maleficarum:"

DEAN: So the Devil may care after all, is that what I'm supposed to believe?

RUBY: I don't believe in the Devil.

DEAN: Wacky night. So let me get this straight, you were human once, you died, you went to Hell, you became a ...

RUBY: Yeah.

DEAN: How long ago?

RUBY: Back when the plague was big.

DEAN: So all of 'em, every damn demon, they were all human once.

RUBY: Everyone I've ever met.

DEAN: Well, they sure don't act like it.

RUBY: Most of them have forgotten what it means, or even that they were. That's what happens when you go to Hell, Dean. That's what Hell is, forgetting what you are.

DEAN: Philosophy lessons from the demon, I'll pass, thanks.

RUBY: It's not philosophy, it's not a metaphor. There's a real fire in the pit, agonies you can't even imagine.

"Ruby my dear," of course this is philosophy, and you're not going to fool us into thinking otherwise.[5] In fact, almost anything can be thought about in philosophical terms, including *Supernatural.* Honestly, what's more philosophical than a demon saying, "I don't believe in the Devil"? Coincidentally, there was a philosopher who was actually accused of being the incarnation of the Devil, Baruch Spinoza (1634–1677). We can excuse Ruby if she doesn't recognize Spinoza, since he came well after her time on Earth. In his *Ethics,* Spinoza conceives of God as the infinite, everything in nature, a view called "Pantheism." But after concluding that God exists, Spinoza concludes that evil does not. Ironically, while many thought of Spinoza as the Devil, he denied the Devil's existence. Spinoza said, "The knowledge of evil is an inadequate knowledge."[6]

The literary theorist Terry Eagleton argues that "inadequate knowledge" is just another way of saying that we use the word "evil" to describe things we don't really understand. Nothing can really be evil just for the sake of it. In *Supernatural,* different villains have different goals, like power, changing society, or sometimes just vengeance, but their goals are never simply to be evil. The demon Crowley, for example, always explains his actions in terms of his quest for power. Lucifer too has his reasons for acting-out, and they aren't to simply be evil. He's actually a frustrated child who's lost the love and attention of his father. Often what appears evil to us is something justifiable or purposeful for the character doing it.

In contrast to Spinoza, journalist Chris Hedges argues that evil is part of human nature and that those who search for an ideal society are destined to create forms of totalitarianism.[7] In his book, *I Don't Believe in Atheists,* Hedges describes people seeking an ideal society as falling into one of two groups, Dogmatic-Bigoted Atheists and Dogmatic-Bigoted Theists. One group wants the eradication of religion and belief in the supernatural, while the other wants the elimination of secularism for a purely religious world view. This rift in the real world resonates with how demons and angels relate in the world of *Supernatural*, especially in Season 5, as we build up to the Apocalypse. Both groups believe their final victory would bring about progress, and neither group has any respect for the other. In addition, angels and demons want to dominate the Earth even if this means eradicating humans in the process.

Forgetting What You Are

Hedges inappropriately blames René Descartes and Immanuel Kant (1724–1804), among others, for the development of a "Godless Religion" led by popular atheists like Richard Dawkins and Sam Harris.[8] As we have seen, Descartes clearly believed in God. And Hedges should actually find a great ally in Kant, who defended a kind of "moral theism" and opposed dogmatic atheism. In his "Lectures on Rational Theology," Kant said:

> Now indeed the belief in a merely possible God as world ruler is obviously the minimum of theology; but is of great enough influence, that for a human being, who already recognizes the necessity of his duties with apodictic certainty, it can call forth his morality. It is quite otherwise with the dogmatic atheist, who directly denies the existence of a God, and who declares it impossible that there is a God at all. Such dogmatic atheists have either never existed, or they are the most evil of human beings. In them all the incentives of morality have fallen away; and it is to these atheists that moral theism stands opposed.[9]

Kant's "moral theism" fits with the view of biologist Joan Roughgarden in her book *Evolution and Christian Faith: Reflections of an Evolutionary Biologist*.[10] Roughgarden argues that evolution is not detached from what God intended, and that the processes involved in evolution are more about cooperation than competition. In *Supernatural*, there are many stories that illustrate the central role played by cooperation in survival. In "Survival of the Fittest" we see that the successful teamwork of Sam, Dean, Castiel, and Meg is essential to beating the leviathans. In fact, Sam and Dean need each other so much that they're practically codependent. Every episode of *Supernatural* contains numerous examples of collaboration necessary for survival. In fact, the loss of Bobby is so traumatic to the maintenance of these relationships and collaborations that he must be replaced by Garth.

As *Supernatural* illustrates, loving relationships don't need to be mutually beneficial; one person may even risk his life to save another person he loves. For example, Corbett saves everyone in "Ghostfacers" as a direct result of his love for Ed. In this case, the homosexual love aids in survival. For her part, Roughgarden argues that, contrary to common belief, the Bible recognizes homosexuals as children of God, including them as equals in God's plan for a better, loving society.[11]

Kant wrote, "There is a being whose existence is prior to the very possibility both of itself and of all things; this being, therefore, is said to exist absolutely necessarily. That being is called God."[12] The God of *Supernatural* sometimes seems to fit this description, but there are also suggestions to the contrary: that God is a finite, palpable character that could die, is dead, or will someday die.

Irish philosopher Gorge Berkeley (1685–1753) believed that the death of God would result in the elimination of everything. While Descartes popularized "I think, therefore I am," Berkeley believed, "God thinks, therefore I am." Berkeley thought that all things exist, because they are perceived. However, it isn't our perception that matters, since our walking out of a room doesn't cause the room to blink out of existence. What matters is that God perceives all things, even if we don't. In other words, if God stops perceiving, then everything would blink out of existence. As a result, God's death would have grave consequences for you and me.

The philosopher Georg Wilhelm Friedrich Hegel (1770–1831) developed Berkeley's idea of God's perception to explain consciousness. Hegel wrote:

> Man has knowledge of God only to the extent that in man God has knowledge of himself. This knowing is God's consciousness of himself, and at the same time it is God's knowledge of man, and this knowing of man by God is man's knowledge of God.[13]

As a result of this circular reasoning, Hegel believed you will only know God if you know yourself. However, knowing yourself isn't as simple as self-reflection or journaling. Hegel believed that the path to knowing yourself requires you to know the history of human society. By knowing more about human history, you become better aware of the people around you, their perspectives, and how you are connected with them. Hegel believed that the more aware you are of this collective reality, the more you are aware of God.

Failing to truly know oneself and failing to be fully aware of this reality is to be distant from God. As Ruby suggests, forgetting what you are or failing to know what you are is what it means to live in Hell. True awareness of your reality and humankind is communion with God. According to Erich Fromm (1900–1980), atheism is not meaningful because it seeks to assert the existence of man by negating God's existence.[14] For both Hegel and Fromm, there is a connection between selfishness and those who deny God. The works of renowned atheist, Richard Dawkins, would seem to support this connection. Dawkins's book, *The Selfish Gene*, promotes a view of nature emphasizing competition. Therein, Dawkins explains that we are survival machines, robot vehicles blindly programmed to preserve the selfish replicators known as genes.[15] According to Dawkins, we exist entirely for the preservation of these genes. We are nothing more than their disposable survival machines. The world of the selfish gene is one of savage competition, ruthless exploitation, and deceit.[16] After more than 30 years, Dawkins's opinion remains relatively unchanged. In his book, *The God Delusion*, he writes, "The logic of Darwinism concludes that the unit in the hierarchy of life which survives and passes through the filter of natural selection will tend to be selfish."[17]

According to Roughgarden, Dawkins has developed a philosophy of universal selfishness, conflict, and lack of empathy, as though this were evident from the study of evolutionary biology.[18] However, many biologists disagree. And philosophers have made progress in conceptualizing team intention, team agency, and collective reason.[19] In a parallel development, the central and defining role of the conductor in music is being contested, allowing for more team agency and collective reason. There are now orchestras without conductors, like New York's orchestra Orpheus[20] and Moscow's Persimfans.[21] These orchestras allow each musician to be an interpreter and team leader. This is a very egalitarian approach to the music, but the real strength of this cooperative design is in the impact of shared and diverse leadership.

Playing without a conductor requires rotating leadership. Different musicians lead different sections for each piece of music played. Eventually, everyone has the opportunity to lead and follow. As a result of this egalitarian design, each member of the orchestra is more aware of the music being played. Each member is less alienated from the group, and they are deeply engaged in their reality, sharing equally in the success or failure of musical performance. Similarly, Sam and Dean share their leadership, attempting to reach some consensus or mutual common ground as to the best course of action.

In fact, an important theme throughout *Supernatural* is that we learn about ourselves by learning about others. If Ruby is right about Hell, then Heaven must be a place of knowing who we are. This leaves Earth, in the middle, as the place of searching and learning what we are. But as Hegel and many other philosophers have tried to teach us, this search is not inside us but in other people. In learning about and celebrating others, we learn about and celebrate God.

Love and Redemption and Every Damn Demon

No doubt, having come from Ruby, it was intended to mess with our heads, but there's still one thing, if true, that should make us particularly uncomfortable. If every damn demon was once human, what kind of God would make a place like Hell?

Since this is a particularly deep question, we'll need to reference a particularly deep episode, "The French Mistake." This creative episode allowed producer Bob Singer to muse about relevant motifs from the show. In particular, Singer refuses to blow off the ending scene where Sam and Dean sit on the Impala and discuss their feelings. For Singer, this scene is the soul of the show, two brothers asking difficult questions, reflecting on their most recent hunt and the battles to come. This ending scene is one of the few places where love, respect, values, and friendships are all open for debate. Often philosophical, the ending scene may hold the key to understanding God in *Supernatural*.

Two brothers finding rest and solace in the company of one another can call to mind Jesus's words from the Book of Matthew, "For where two or three are gathered together in my name, there am I in the midst of them."[22] You don't need to accept the New Testament to see that the love between the two brothers is a constant in the series. And God does claim to be love. If Sam and Dean are gathered together in the name of love, then God is present. Furthermore, we know that Sam and Dean don't always share the same values. But their differences don't seem to substantially change the love they have for one another.

Opposing values don't necessarily form insurmountable obstacles in a relationship. Consider what we can learn by contrasting the relationship of Michael and Lucifer with that of Sam and Dean. The God of *Supernatural* wants loving relationships above all else. Even after Michael and Lucifer say they love one another, their father allows them to be pushed into the Cage of Hell after they aren't willing to back down from their absolute beliefs about right and wrong. Neither is able to change, neither is capable of the forgiveness and redemption necessary for a lasting, loving relationship.

Sam and Dean handle very serious disagreements differently than Michael and Lucifer. In "Bloodlust," we see an early example of the impasse between Dean's drive to kill every monster and Sam's hope that not all monsters are purely evil. Sam has to hope for this, since he is concerned that he too will need redemption if he becomes a monster someday. This possibility of redemption grants Sam some hope, but it does nothing for Dean. In "The Girl Next Door," Dean stabs and kills Sam's childhood friend simply because she is a monster. Even though the brothers get angry with one another, they manage to transcend their differences and forgive their extreme offenses to one another's values. They still manage to allow for reconciliation and redemption.

Now, if we really are to learn anything about God from these themes in the show, how exactly does unwavering love, forgiveness, and redemption stack up to a God that allows for people to go to Hell and become demons? This issue becomes particularly prominent as Dean and Sam may have a chance to close the gates of Hell forever. But is that what God would want? Are the gates of Hell supposed to be closed? If Ruby was right and every demon was once human, then closing the gates of Hell denies them the chance to atone for their sins. It prevents a chance for redemption. Castiel is certainly concerned about atoning for his time as "God," so why not demons? Is Castiel on much better footing than they are?

The Philosopher John Locke (1632–1704) argued that the idea of redemption could be arrived at in principle by the same sort of reasoning that arrives at the idea of God.[23] Since closing the gates of Hell means denying demons the opportunity to become human again through redemption, closing the gates of Hell is contrary to God's nature. In other words, it's not Hell that is contrary to God's nature, but the prohibition on redemption that would be caused by closing Hell's gates. Only those truly dogmatic in their beliefs are separated from God, and there is a special place in Hell for them, the Cage.

Notes

1. For now, I'm ignoring that Chuck may be God. While we are led to believe that he is, it's also reasonable to doubt this.
2. "Dark Side of the Moon."
3. René Descartes, *Oeuvres de Descartes Vol. VII—Meditations with Objections and Replies*, ed. Charles Adam and Paul Tannery (Paris: Vrin, 1974–1989), 68–69. Trans. by Lawrence Nolan and Alan Nelson in *The Blackwell Guide to Descartes' Meditations*, ed. Stephen Gaukroger (Oxford: Blackwell, 2006), 113.
4. René Descartes in Harry G. Frankfurt, *Demons, Dreamers, and Madmen The Defense of Reason in Descartes's Meditations* (Princeton: Princeton University Press, 2008), 118.
5. "Ruby My Dear" is a jazz ballad composed by Thelonious Monk (1917–1982) and superbly played by John Coltrane (1926–1967). Some say that whenever these musicians are listened to, God is there.

6. Baruch Spinoza, Ethics Proposition LXIV, in Edwin Curley, *A Spinoza Reader: the Ethics and Other Works* (Princeton: Princeton University Press, 1994), 234.
7. C. Hedges, *I Don't Believe in Atheists* (London: Continuum, 2008).
8. Ibid., 17.
9. Immanuel Kant, "Lectures on Rational Theology," in Peter Byrne, *Kant on God* (Burlington: Ashgate, 2007), 91.
10. Joan Roughgarden, *Evolution and Christian Faith—Reflections of an Evolutionary Biologist* (London: Island Press, 2006).
11. Joan Roughgarden, *The Genial Gene* (London: University of California Press, 2009), 101–124, 238.
12. Immanuel Kant, Preposition VII of Principiorum Primorum Cognitionis Metaphysicae—Nova Dilucidatio (1755), in F.E. England, *Kant's Conception of God* (New York: Humanities Press, 1968), 224.
13. Friedrich Hegel, *Vorlesungen über die Philosophie der Religion* (2 vols., Frankfurt a/M: Suhrkamp, 1969), 117 in Quentin Lauer, *Hegel's Concept of God* (New York: State University of New York Press, 1982), 213.
14. Erich Fromm, *Marx's Concept Of Man* (New York: Frederick Ungar Publishing Co. 1961), 140.
15. Richard Dawkins, *The Selfish Gene* (Oxford: Oxford University Press, 1976).
16. Ibid.
17. Richard Dawkins, *The God Delusion* (New York: Bantam Press, 2008).
18. Joan Roughgarden, *The Genial Gene—Deconstructing Darwinian Selfishness* (London: University of California Press, 2009), 5, 178.
19. Philosophers such as Michael Bratman, "Shared Intention," *Ethics* 104 (1993): 97–113; Robert Sugden, "Thinking as a Team: Toward an Explanation of Nonselfish Behavior," *Social Philosophy Policy* 10 (1993): 69–89; Robert Sugden, "Team Preferences," *Economics Philosophy* 16 (2000): 175–204; Robert Sugden, "The Logic of Team Reasoning," *Philosophical Explorations* 6 (2003): 165–181; Natalie Gold, Framing and Decision Making: A Reason-Based Approach (D.Phil thesis, University of Oxford, 2005); Michael Bacharach, *Beyond Individual Choice: Teams and Frames in Game Theory* (Princeton: Princeton University Press, 2006); Natalie Gold and Robert Sugden, "Theories of Team Agency," in *Rationality and Commitment*, ed. Peter Fabienne and Hans Bernhard Schmid (Oxford: Oxford University Press, 2008), 280–312.

20. Harvey Seifter and Peter Economy, *Leadership Ensemble—Lessons in Collaborative Management from the World's Only Conductorless Orchestra* (New York: Henry Holt and Co, 2002).

21. Danilo Chaib, "Спиной к публике, лицом к музыке" (Back to the audience, facing the music) Музокно Magazine, www.musokno.ru/events/?catalogue_id=22&item_id=2129> (accessed March 20, 2013).

22. Jesus in Matthew 18:20, *The Bible: Authorized King James Version* (New York: Oxford University Press, 2008).

23. John Locke, in Jeremy Waldron, *God, Locke, and Equality—Christian Foundations of John Locke's Political Thought* (Cambridge: Cambridge University Press, 2002), 208.

Part Four
IT'S SUPERNATURAL

Chapter 13

Naturally Supernatural

James Blackmon with Galen A. Foresman

What is it to be supernatural? We can all think of examples. A ghost is a supernatural being that is typically described as capable of appearing to, speaking to, and even doing harm to a person. But it is also described as a being that you cannot touch or affect in the usual ways. The magic spell, in which words, gestures, and thoughts mysteriously bring about significant physical effects, is another good example. "Incendio," when said by Harry Potter, causes flames to shoot forth, clearly a supernatural ability. Similarly, Sam's ability to cast out demons without an exorcism during the fourth and fifth seasons of *Supernatural* is also a supernatural ability. A particular favorite of mine is holy water, which is presumably indistinguishable from other samples of water except that it has many powers, including the power to burn the flesh of vampires and demons alike. These are the kinds of things that we call "supernatural," and they all play prominent roles in the series *Supernatural*. But what unites them? And what, if anything, distinguishes them from the natural? In short, what is it that makes them supernatural?

Supernatural and Philosophy: Metaphysics and Monsters ... for Idjits, First Edition.
Edited by Galen A. Foresman.
© 2013 John Wiley & Sons, Inc. Published 2013 by John Wiley & Sons, Inc.

Fiction, Myth, and Weirdness

The answer cannot be that they are matters of fiction. After all, many fictional things are not "supernatural." Close friend and confidant to Sam and Dean, Bobby Singer, doesn't exist, nor does his ball cap. But, neither Bobby nor his hat is supernatural. In fact, many things in *Supernatural* are purely fictional, like some towns they visit, swanky hotel rooms they crash in, websites they browse, and other human characters they interact with. Obviously, this is of no surprise, but the point is that even though their world is brimming with supernatural things, we would not call everything in their world "supernatural." Nor can the answer be that supernatural things are simply things we don't believe in. European naturalists were once skeptical of the existence of gorillas, but that didn't make all the gorillas in the world supernatural.

To say that something is supernatural is akin to saying that it *just isn't natural*, but we shouldn't confuse that with thinking that something is simply *weird*. Lots of things seem weird at first, but we humans don't think of them as supernatural. Just consider moon landings, atomic bombs, holographic stickers from gumball machines, velociraptors, black holes, self-replicating proteins, and parasitic twins. None of these things actually defy nature, and they all fit our understanding of the natural world, even if most people once didn't expect them to.

So the "supernatural" can't just be what we know to be fictional or what we think doesn't exist. Nor can it be what we find to be weird. So far, we know something about what *being supernatural* isn't.

Isn't This What Dictionaries Are For?

I'm going to unabashedly resort to a time-honored, though clichéd, convention of essay writing—reporting the dictionary definition. But my reason for doing this isn't merely to find a rhetorical stepping stone. I want to show that our problem of figuring out what it means to be supernatural isn't simply cleared up by referring to a dictionary. As the twentieth-century philosopher Willard Van Orman Quine (1908–2000) famously explained, dictionary definitions cannot play the definitive role we sometimes expect of them. This is because the lexicographers, in putting together their dictionary, rely on empirical research. In other words, lexicographers try to figure out definitions for most words from how those words are used. But those words are used by us, the very people the lexicographers hope to sell dictionaries to. How, then, can we rely upon the lexicographers to tell us what our words mean if they rely upon us to tell them what our words mean, all so they can tell us what out words mean?

We seem to be dealing with some kind of paradox or vicious circle here.[1] Ultimately, though, we can rest assured that this paradox isn't going to bring about the Apocalypse, because definitions, like seat allocations on the subway, just get done. We print them, we read them, we use them, and our life and language continues unabated. But also like seat allocations on the subway, definitions don't always get done well, which is why we'll need to be somewhat skeptical of their absolute authority on the meaning of the word "supernatural."

My *New Lexicon Webster's Dictionary of the English Language* reports that "supernatural," used as an adjective, means "not able to be explained in terms of the known laws which govern the material universe." On the other hand, my *New Shorter Oxford English Dictionary* provides these two entries, neither of which agree with Webster:

1. That which transcends or is above nature; of or pertaining to a supposed force or system above the laws of nature.
2. Beyond the natural or ordinary; unnaturally or extraordinarily great.

Let's start with *Webster's* definition. Currently, the universe expands at a rate unexplainable by the known laws of physics. Based on *Webster's* definition, this rate of expansion must be supernatural. A former world religions teacher of mine insisted that science could not entirely explain how a hummingbird flies. I've always been very skeptical of this claim, but if he's right, then *Webster's* definition is committed to categorizing the flight of hummingbirds as part of the supernatural. Of course, it seems the day may come—if it hasn't come already—when scientists figure out how hummingbirds fly. On that day, according to *Webster*, the flight of a hummingbird loses its supernatural status. For *Webster*, the problem is that *being supernatural* is a mere tracker of human knowledge and ignorance, like *being obvious* or *being confusing*. It recedes over time as we learn and understand new things.

Turning now to *Oxford*'s definition, *being supernatural* doesn't depend on what we know or don't know about the laws of the material universe. Thankfully, hummingbirds are safely excluded from the realm of the supernatural, even if we don't fully understand them. Furthermore, *Oxford*'s definition correctly groups ghosts and magical incantations among the things that are supernatural. So far, so good for *Oxford*, but really, the problem I suggested earlier begins with the simple fact that these dictionaries give substantially different definitions. A thing may be categorized as "supernatural" according to *Webster* but not according to *Oxford*. And while, admittedly, I do have an intuitive preference for *Oxford*'s definition, the deeper problem is that there's no obvious way to really determine which definition is better.

Ultimately, I think all of these problems result from the concept of *being supernatural*, which is far more elusive than our dictionary definitions have led us to believe. In fact, I'm suggesting here that this concept threatens to be nonsense when we try to take it too seriously—as perhaps I am doing right now.

Small Comforts from the Causal Nexus

Oxford stays true to the etymology of the word "supernatural," which is "above nature." This may be a helpful starting place, since now all we have to do is determine what it is to be part of nature, and then say that *being supernatural* is being above or beyond that. Again, so far, so good. So now what is it to be part of nature? And what exactly is nature? Is Advil, a human artifact, part of nature?

We often distinguish the products of civilization from nature, but surely *Oxford* doesn't mean to suggest that Advil be placed alongside Goofer Dust, Quincunx, and other assorted Hoodoo. Given that, it seems to make better sense to keep Advil among the natural by understanding "natural" to mean anything made entirely of natural things, even products of civilization.

Perhaps we could understand "nature" to include all the physical things following physical laws. But are we talking about the physical things and laws as we currently understand them with our admittedly incomplete scientific knowledge? Or, are we talking about the actual physical things that exist and the laws that govern them, regardless of whether we currently know or understand these things? In other words, are we including in the "physical things following physical laws" all the stuff we would have discovered in some ultimate utopia of scientific omniscience?[2] If we take the first option, using language of "as we currently understand them," then we risk ending up with the embarrassments encountered by *Webster's* definition. For, if the history of science is any indication, we will make more substantial discoveries in the future and not the least among them will be discoveries that some of our currently held scientific beliefs are mistaken. As a result, according to this first understanding of the physical things and laws that make up nature, all future discoveries are automatically in the realm of the supernatural, because they don't belong among the physical things and laws as we currently understand them.

So in an effort to avoid *Webster's* mistake, we had better go with the second option, understanding "nature" to include the *actual* physical things and laws, not just those we think we know and understand. From there, we can conclude that the supernatural includes everything beyond that. Of course, we've already admitted we don't really have perfect knowledge of the natural world as it is, so it's not clear that this way of thinking about *actual* physical things and laws really rules out anything. This could be a problem.

Suppose, for example, that in 30 years some future scientists—say, Drs. Ed Zeddmore and Harry Spangler—publish a scientific study providing actual scientific evidence that ghosts are among the things that exist and are governed by physical laws.[3] Maybe these scientists and others like them learn to capture ghosts within rings of salt and then run experiments on them. And maybe we come to learn from these experiments that ghosts are comprised of electromagnetic systems that somehow manage to have enough physical integrity and complexity to think and communicate like people. If that happened, then ghosts would not be above and beyond nature. They would be a part of nature, and thus not supernatural. The unfortunate result of understanding the concept of supernatural in this way is that our paradigm examples of the supernatural might all turn out to be just plain natural, and therefore not very supernatural at all. Ghosts might just be natural. Ghosts!

As yet another alternative, perhaps we should understand the natural as whatever is caught up in the causal nexus of this world, making the supernatural whatever lies beyond that nexus. In other words, the natural would include anything and everything that causally interacts together, and the supernatural would be everything else that can't participate in all these causal interactions. For example, anything that takes up physical space must causally interact with other things that take up space.

While admittedly small, there is at least some comfort knowing that natural assailants take up physical space. As a result, natural assailants can't share the same physical space with other things like hands, doors, and blunt objects. This simple fact allows you to push natural assailants away, if you're strong enough. It allows you to barricade yourself safely away, if you're fast enough, and it even allows of you to bash assailants' heads in, if you're armed enough. But ghosts, paragons of the supernatural, lack this comforting feature of filling space. Your hands pass through them; they pass effortlessly through your heavy locked doors; and those weapons you were hoping to defend yourself with are just deadweight so far as ghosts are concerned—unless, of course, you've loaded them with rock salt or iron. As Shakespeare's Marcellus says of the ghost in *Hamlet*, "it is as the air, invulnerable, / And our vain blows malicious mockery." (Marcellus didn't know about the rock salt and iron.)

Getting Literally Too Literal

Typically, and as in *Hamlet*, the ghost is not entirely removed from our causal nexus. Otherwise, how would we know about him? When Hamlet and his friends see his father's ghost (whom Shakespeare calls Ghost), that's only possible if their eyes collected light that had been reflected, refracted, or emitted from the Ghost. Had the Ghost not been there, their eyes would have been affected by light differently.[4] So clearly, the Ghost and earthly light causally interact. And when the Ghost speaks to Hamlet, the Ghost somehow sends sound waves through the atmosphere, vibrating his ghostly vocal chords. The end result is the vibration of the tympanic membrane in Hamlet's ear, thereby allowing him to hear spooky things like, "The serpent that did sting thy father's life / Now wears his crown," which is, as I'm sure you know, possibly the most causally potent moment of the play, if not of Hamlet's life.

Of course, Bobby deals with the same exact sort of communication problems after he dies in "Death's Door," and the obvious lesson to be learned from Bobby's experience is that ghosts typically *do* fit into the causal nexus. They just have to work really hard at it. What then can we make of the definition according to which "supernatural" means strictly beyond the causal nexus? Well, according to that definition, even though Bobby's dead and free to walk through walls, the fact that he can also causally interact with Sam, Dean, and other objects would mean he's not at all supernatural. He's a natural thing that's just very weird, given our limited understanding of the natural world.

Alternatively, we could maintain our causal nexus understanding of the natural, and simply embrace the blasphemous view that *Supernatural's* writers messed up. Ghosts, if they were to be truly supernatural entities according to the definition we're considering, could not affect us at all, nor could we affect them. If they existed, they'd float about completely independent of this world. They couldn't harm us. They couldn't even scare us. They couldn't have any causal interaction with us at all. Even the most rage-filled, blood-thirsty, howling banshee of this kind could make no appearances, creak no floorboards, and rustle no curtains in our world. And it couldn't hear or sense us either. If ghosts like this exist, entombed in their causally isolated parallel universe, they can make no difference good or bad in our lives and we can't make any such differences in their non-lives.

I'm inclined to reject this option simply on the basis that it's boring, but really, there's a better reason to reject it. This understanding of the natural and supernatural fails to account for our prototypical examples from the start—ghosts, spells, and holy water—all of which are supposed to causally interact with our world, while still counting among the supernatural. In other words, by this way of thinking, the ghosts in *Supernatural* are actually natural, and any truly supernatural entities are irrelevant.

So far, we've seen that things that are causally relevant to us, however strange, don't really count as supernatural under any definition that respects the etymology of the word. We've also seen that taking the etymology too literally, as we just did, leads to an intolerable conception of ghosts, since they can't do anything to us, they can't be detected, and they can't even be scary. At this point in our philosophical journey, we have a lot to be disappointed about. But I bring you good news and glad tidings—we now know exactly where we're going with our concept of supernatural.

We know that our conception of supernatural must allow for a ghost to be "immaterial enough" to pass through your bedroom door but "material enough" to constrict your throat with its cold, clammy hand. Yes, we must have a conception of supernatural that allows for transcending the causal nexus in some ways but not others, allowing ghosts to pass effortlessly through walls, while walking firmly (for some reason) upon floors. We need supernatural things that can causally interact with us, and yet defy the laws of the natural world at the same time. At long last, we have our definition of the supernatural: Something is supernatural if it can, on occasion, transcend the world of material interaction.

Now all we need is a coherent understanding of the world of material interaction. Otherwise, we haven't really solved our problem of defining supernatural if all we've really done is add phrases like, "transcend the world of material interaction." We need to explain those phrases, so that we're sure they don't result in the same problems had by previous definitions.

Being Two With Nature[5]

In his *Meditations on First Philosophy*, René Descartes (1596–1650) argued that the mind (by which he meant the same thing as the soul) was an immaterial thing that causally interacted with the material body. A man ahead of his time, Descartes was working on a theory very similar to the one we're working on here, which is known as *interactionist substance dualism*. It's been dubbed "interactionist" by philosophers, because the mind and body causally interact. The body lets the mind sense the world, and the mind guides the body's voluntary motor activity. The term "substance" is used because Descartes thought that the world is composed of two fundamental types of substances: (1) extended material bodies, and (2) non-extended immaterial minds. Neither substance is a feature of the other in the sense that, say, a ripple is a feature of the water. Each is a thing that could exist independently of the other. A substance *underlies* its features and can go on existing even when it loses particular features. Thus, Descartes understood one of his tasks to be explaining how immaterial things, like the mind, can interact with material things, like our brains and bodies. He may as well have claimed to be figuring out how ghosts interact with people.

It's easy to see how material things interact with each other. After all, they are, by their very essence as things filling space, things that cannot merge into each other. As we noted in our discussion of the causal nexus, if one material thing occupies a space, no other material thing can occupy that space without pushing it out of the way. And this would have been a common conception of causal interaction in Descartes' time. The natural world can be seen as one of matter in motion, with plenty of collisions. The supernatural, then, goes beyond this picture in some way.

Thus far, we have a view that is very common to many religions and belief systems across the world and throughout history. And it's perfect for *Supernatural*. On such a view, concepts like the after-life, the channeling of spirits, out-of-body experiences, and demonic possession are perfectly conceivable. In each case, the interactive links between two substances, body and spirit, are cut or rear-ranged. In death and in out-of-body experiences, the spirit breaks free of the body (becomes *disembodied*), either to pass on into some afterlife, to return eventually to the body, or to roam the natural world. Mediums, who channel spirits, allow other spirits to gain interactive access to their bodies, so the spirits can speak with the medium's voice and see with the medium's eyes. Possession occurs when a spirit gets too much (or total) control of your body. In some cases, your spirit rides along watching helplessly, while in others, your spirit loses its connection to your body and you are none the wiser.

Interactionist substance dualism is actually quite a common view. But Descartes offered reasons beyond its popularity for thinking of the world this way. Here is a very quick version of the kind of reasoning Descartes pursued:

> I can imagine myself having another body or even no body at all. After all, in the midst of a dream, I've believed many things that turned out to be false. I might have dreamed, as the Chinese philos-opher Zhuangzi is said to have dreamed, that I was a butterfly and truly believed it in the moment, and yet, been totally wrong. For all I know, life is like one long dream, and my current impression of having a human body (along with my memories of that body) is simply false. Thus, the human body and indeed all the physical world is *doubtable*.

This fact about the "doubtability" of the physical world is impor-tant because it's what separates the mind and body into distinct entities. While the body's existence can be doubted, the mind's existence cannot.

Why does Descartes think the body is doubtable whereas the mind is not? Well, go ahead and try to doubt that you have a mind. If you failed, that's OK; it's only because you can't doubt that you have a mind. No one can. After all, the mind is the very thing doing the doubting. Your mind can doubt the existence of the body, but your mind cannot doubt its own existence because doing so presupposes the existence of the doubter, that is the mind. To put it another way, no mind could believe it existed, when it did not. Pure logic appears to dictate that no super-being, no matter how powerful, could bring that about. As Dean discovered in "What Is and What Should Never Be," a djinn can change everything you think you know about the physical world, but even he can't cause you to falsely believe you exist. After all, you have to exist to believe anything.

Here, Descartes achieves certainty of the existence of his own mind, despite his willingness to doubt everything that could possibly be doubted. And here, Descartes finds the inspiration for his famous, "Cogito ergo sum," which translates into the very popular, "I think, therefore I am."

But Descartes is quick to concede that he doesn't know much else about his existence. Despite the way things appear, perhaps he doesn't really have a body (or perhaps he's in the Matrix). But what he does know is that so long as he believes, wonders, and doubts, his mind must exist. So the mind, Descartes finds, must be distinct from the physical body, which is a thing that can be doubted. We now have reason, other than the fact that it's a popular view, to believe in substance dualism. We can conclude that there are two basic things in this world—immaterial minds and material bodies—but now we must explain exactly how these things interact.

Obviously, or so thought Descartes, these two substances causally interact. For, it is the mind that experiences physical life and commands physical actions, and there would be no physical life or actions without the body. When, for example, the eye or some other physical sense organ receives a physical stimulus, eventually that message must reach the immaterial mind if *you* are to have the corresponding experience. And when you choose to raise your hand, that signal must reach your material body if you and your mind are to will that hand raising.

Descartes elaborates this interaction in his *The Passions of the Soul* under the section eloquently titled, *There Is a Little Gland in the Brain Where the Soul Exercises Its Functions More Particularly Than in the Other Parts of the Body*. He begins by noting that people commonly think the brain or the heart is the part of the body that is most sensitive to the activity of the soul:

> But on carefully examining the matter I think I have clearly established that the part of the body in which the soul directly exercises its functions is not the heart at all, or the whole of the brain. It is rather the innermost part of the brain, which is a certain very small gland situated in the middle of the brain's substance and suspended above the passage through which the spirits in the brain's anterior cavities communicate with those in its posterior cavities. The slightest movements on the part of this gland may alter very greatly the course of these spirits, and conversely any change, however slight, taking place in the course of the spirits may do much to change the movements of the gland.

Descartes is referring to what we now call the pineal gland, and his reasoning follows in his next section, *How We Know That This Gland Is the Principle Seat of the Soul*. But he begins with the basic observation that all other parts of the brain are doubled:

> as also are all the organs of our external senses—eyes, hands, ears and so on. But in so far as we have only one single thought about a given object at any given time, there must necessarily be some place where the two images coming through the eyes, or the two impressions coming from a single object through the double organs of any other sense, can come together in a single image or impression before reaching the soul, so that they do not present to it two objects instead of one. We can easily imagine that these images or other impressions are unified in this gland by means of the spirits which fill the cavities of the brain. But they cannot exist united in this way in any other place in the body except as a result of their being united in this gland.

Thus, Descartes believed it was the pineal gland through which the soul directed the body and by which the soul was influenced to receive the sense impressions the body receives. We can easily extend his reasoning to imagine that other souls might manage to get hold of our pineal glands, thereby possessing us, and that mediums voluntarily temporarily relinquish control of their pineal glands. We can see how out-of-body experiences and life after the death of the body become intelligible. We can push this view even further. Once it is allowed that some physical objects are mysteriously affected by immaterial minds and vice-versa, the possibility arises that other physical objects can be so affected. Perhaps some spirits can physically affect the air, so as to become visible, and perhaps water, when appropriately treated by a priest, becomes holy, somehow gaining the disposition to burn the flesh of vampires.

A Science of the Supernatural

Descartes' view is not just a philosophical speculation; it is also a scientific hypothesis. Although Descartes' reasons for dualism are based primarily in deep philosophical meditation, his reason for identifying the pineal gland as the seat of the soul is based in his investigation of the human brain where Descartes finds an anatomical explanation for some obvious facts about human perception. So, he's trying to unite what we know about the brain with what we know about the mind.

But what makes Descartes' view truly scientific is that it is testable by observation.[6] Recall that he held that the soul interacts with the pineal gland and that the pineal gland influences the body with slight movements. This is a hypothesis that can be tested in two parts. First, simply observe movements in the pineal gland followed by changes in the body, in order to see if the pineal gland influences the body in the way Descartes suggested. The second observation, however, is more important for our purposes. Descartes appears to be committed to the idea that these slight movements of the pineal gland appear to originate from nowhere. That is to say, the gland seems to be affected by something we can't detect, since what's really affecting it is the mind, which is non-physical.

To illustrate this point, think about when you intentionally make a fist. The fist forms as a result of muscle contractions in your hands and arms, which in turn result from stimulation by nerves, which have carried an electrochemical signal from the brain.[7] According to Descartes' hypothesis, this signal originates in the immaterial mind, which controls the pineal gland like a pilot controls an airplane. But unlike the pilot in the plane, the mind itself is not directly observable. We might see the pineal gland move or change, but we couldn't ever see what's causing this. Thus, we'd be finding energy coming from—for all we knew scientifically—out of nowhere. The pineal gland would be the point in the causal nexus of the human body where physical things seemed to happen *for no scientifically observable reason.*

Recalling our current working definition of "supernatural" as something that can transcend the world of material interaction, this would count as being supernatural. In testing Descartes' hypothesis regarding the pineal gland, there were two parts that needed testing. We noted that everything that happens as a result of the pineal gland affecting the rest of the body was scientifically observable and explainable. This is the world of material interaction. On the other hand, we noted that everything that happened prior to the pineal gland's being affected was unobservable. The pineal gland would appear to be affected out of nowhere, and this is what the supernatural looks like when it *transcends* the world of material substance through causal interaction. Now, not only do we have a definition of supernatural that fits with the typical usage of the word, but it's a definition that allows for indirect scientific evidence of its existence through observations of the natural material world. As we've seen, other conceptions of supernatural haven't allowed for this.

Unfortunately, though, Descartes, was flat-out wrong about the pineal gland. According to contemporary scientific understanding, the pineal gland just secretes melatonin and regulates sleep.[8] However, this is only a pressing reason to reject the idea that it is specifically the pineal gland that is the seat of the mind. It is not a defeat of interactionist substance dualism in general. For all we know, the mind works its immaterial magic elsewhere in the brain or somewhere else in the body (perhaps at multiple points), and science has yet to discover where. Most neuroscientists are not holding their breath on this one, and admittedly, neither am I. But it is at least an open possibility.

We can easily imagine the conditions under which rational scientists would be convinced either way on the existence of a non-material mind that is separate from the body.[9] The conditions we find in *Supernatural* would certainly weigh heavily in favor of some form of interactionist substance dualism. And if we were to encounter conditions like these (and we could dispense with the possibility they were the product of an elaborate hoax), it would be scientifically irresponsible to reject the idea that there were non-material agents affecting our material world. The rational response would be to accept such non-material agents along with an equally rational implication: we too, being ultimately the spirits who causally interact with our material bodies, are supernatural.[10]

Notes

1. Indeed, Quine preferred to liken it to a "closed curve in space"; apparently "circle" was somehow misleading.
2. Long ago, the philosopher of science, Carl Hempel, confronted much the same problem, known now as Hempel's Dilemma. What is it to assert that everything is physical? Is it to hold that everything falls under today's physics? This would make physicalism a naïve and surely false view. Is it then, on the other hand, to hold that everything falls under some ideal physics waiting in the future? This would make physicalism a trivial view. We don't know what a final physics would look like, and so it rules nothing out.
3. The linguist Noam Chomsky, for instance, finds the distinction between the physical and the non-physical to be vacuous since any scientifically discovered things will be incorporated among those recognized as physical.
4. Or had Ghost been merely a figment of the imagination, it's hard to see how four sentinels and then later a fifth person, Hamlet himself, all happened to have the same figment in their separate and independently operating imaginations. Also, we as audience members can assume we are shown what is, not what is imagined. So the appearance of Ghost is part of what is, while, for comparison, Macbeth's floating dagger, being a figment of his imagination, typically does not appear in stage productions of *Macbeth*.
5. Acknowledgments to Woody Allen.
6. The twentieth-century philosopher of science, Karl Popper, is celebrated for having used falsifiability to draw a clean line between

science and pseudoscience. What makes a conjecture scientific is not whether it has lots of evidence in its favor, but whether we know what would falsify it. Scientific conjectures then rule a lot of possible observations out—no excuses. They dare to hold themselves to obvious tests. Pseudoscience on the other hand makes room for all kinds of vague variations and contingencies, so many that it ends up saying hardly anything at all. The astronomer predicts a star will appear in a small region of the sky during a specific brief period of time, putting that prediction to a straightforward test of observation, one that can clearly falsify or corroborate it depending on what is observed. The astrologer, on the other hand, predicts that you will have a hard week (or day) soon, real soon … if not physically challenging, then at least mentally challenging … or perhaps challenging in the sense that it is so physically and mentally unchallenging you will be challenged to find something interesting about it. What has this "prediction" ruled out? What could happen that would prove it false?

7. Descartes would call these signals "animal spirits," and scientists nowadays sometimes snicker at what sounds like an appeal to the occult. However, there is no reason to think he meant anything beyond "animating influences," which is in fact what these electro-chemical signals are. To be fair to Descartes, he was just naming them functionally, admitting he didn't know much more about them than what they obviously did.

8. A stubborn dualist might respond, "Aha! Since in sleep we become unconscious and lose control of our bodies, this is actually some further support for Descartes' view! We now have a mechanism to explain what connects and disconnects the mind and body!" This is a tantalizing view, but it does not account for the fact that motor signals do not radiate from the pineal gland, nor do all sensory signals culminate there.

9. In this regard, Cartesian dualism distinguishes itself from a variety of newer, but also more boring, forms of dualism which admit of no scientific test.

10. Many thanks to Galen Foresman for helping provide me with useful examples from the show, *Supernatural*.

Chapter 14

Masculinity and Supernatural Love

Stacey Goguen

DEAN: Bitch.
SAM: Jerk.

Sam and Dean battle more supernatural creatures than you can shake a stake at, but there's one thing that scares them more than any monster—"love." Over the years, Sam and Dean have saved the world a few times, but they still can't express their feelings very well. Insults are usually expressions of antagonism and hostility, but for the Winchesters they often mask affection.[1] Though they freely call each other "bitch" and "jerk," the L-word rarely escapes their lips. As we'll see, though, love is central to their lives as brothers, hunters, and men.

The Warrior

MICHAEL: I'm a good son, and I have my orders.
LUCIFER: But you don't have to follow them.

Supernatural illustrates two dominant ideals of masculinity, the warrior and the sovereign. The warrior is strong and powerful, as exemplified by Dean and the Archangel Michael. The sovereign is

Supernatural and Philosophy: Metaphysics and Monsters ... for Idjits, First Edition.
Edited by Galen A. Foresman.
© 2013 John Wiley & Sons, Inc. Published 2013 by John Wiley & Sons, Inc.

independent and autonomous, as exemplified by Sam and Lucifer. Strictly speaking, though, there's nothing necessarily masculine about these ideals.[2] Women can embody them as well. However, in *Supernatural*, the role of the warrior is often associated with the role of the hunter. In the first episode of the series, Sam points out that they "were raised like warriors" by their father, John Winchester. Hunters often assume they must be capable fighters in order to be proper hunters. When Bobby loses the use of his legs in "The Curious Case Of Dean Winchester," he laments, "I ain't a hunter no more. I'm useless." In fact, Bobby can still outwit, out-maneuver, and outdraw many supernatural baddies. But because he's no longer able-bodied, he can't conceive of himself as a hunter.

Of course, some hunters are women, so why would the hunter/warrior ideal be masculine? For starters, there aren't many women hunters, so they tend to be exceptions to the rule. Beyond that, they aren't presented as being as capable at the job as men. For instance, Ellen, Jo, Tamara, and Gwen are all saved by male hunters at some crucial point. Last but not least, there's an unspoken code of ethics in *Supernatural*, as well as in the real world, that implies men are responsible for saving the world and all its *damsels*. It's called, "chivalry."

Chivalry is a code of ethics requiring people to protect those who cannot protect themselves. Feminist philosophers such as Simone de Beauvoir (1908–1986) have discussed the ethics of *protectors* and *protected wards*, arguing that though there's nothing that demands men be the protectors, cultural narratives almost always skew that way. The result is we end up associating being a pro-tector with masculinity. Indeed, Sam and Dean could be poster-boys for this chivalric assumption.

In the first season, Dean tells Sam that the family business is about saving people, not just hunting monsters. By Season 2, it's Sam reminding Dean that their primary role isn't just killing, but destroying evil before it hurts innocent people. In fact, chivalry explains the brothers' opposition to the angels in Season 5. In killing Lucifer, the angels would bring about the deaths of billions of people. The chivalrous Sam and Dean feel compelled to defeat Lucifer without all that collateral damage.

Dean's sense of self is especially tied to his role as protector. Originally, he describes his job as saving people, but eventually, this description fails to satisfy him. In "What Is and What Should Never Be," he laments over his father's grave, "I know what you'd say … Your happiness for all those people's lives, no contest. But why? Why is it my *job* to save these people?" In "Swan Song," Dean answers his own question, asserting that protecting Sam is not just his job, "but more than that, it's who I am." This shift in Dean's attitude demonstrates that chivalry isn't just a part of Dean's job; it's an expression of his selfhood, his manhood.

In addition to being a physically strong and able protector, the warrior ideal requires psychological strength. The warrior hones the skills of mind and spirit in addition to body. Dean, Sam, and Bobby repeatedly face psychological and emotional assaults, and they interpret any failure on this front as a failure in manliness. For instance, when Dean calls Bobby for emotional support in "Weekend at Bobby's," he apologizes, "… forget it. I mean I'm baring my soul like a freaking girl and you've got stuff to do." In similar fashion, Bobby chastises Dean in "Lucifer Rising" for feeling rejected, "Well, boo hoo, I am so sorry your feelings are hurt, princess!" Since Dean more strongly identifies with the warrior ideal than Sam, his being perceived as emotionally vulnerable is particularly threatening to masculinity. Furthermore, Sam becomes a near-perfect hunter when he loses his soul and all those pesky emotions that came with it.

The Sovereign

The masculine ideal of the sovereign is a person who strives to be free above all else. The sovereign has what Isaiah Berlin (1909–1997) described as both positive and negative liberty. Negative liberty is freedom *from* things, like restrictions, restraints, obstacles, coercion, or force. In this sense, the sovereign is independent, free from influence. From the show's outset, Sam is a prime example of the sovereign ideal. He left the family for college, sick of following his father's orders.

Positive liberty is the freedom *to do* things. For the sovereign, this means having the unfettered ability to choose goals and accomplish them. The loss of Sam's soul frees him to achieve goals without remorse or regret. He can doggedly pursue his goals without worrying about collateral damage. In this sense, many hunters throughout the series speak of intimate social networks as liabilities. Loved ones can slow hunters down, reduce their options, and burden them with extra considerations.

The sovereign doesn't need to be a hermit, though. The philosopher Thomas Hobbes (1588–1679) is best known for arguing that an absolute sovereign is necessary for stable government. Legal scholar, Edward Coke (1552–1634) noted that every British man's home is his castle—making him the sovereign of his family. This idea later influenced American law, as well. In fact, this notion of the head of a household being an absolute monarch still predominates in American culture. A man saying, "In my house …" harkens back to this idea of his will being the law of the land, or at least, the law of the home.

The sovereign values his own mind, intellect, and will, freeing him pursue his own desires. In this sense, the masculine sovereign is similar to Friedrich Nietzsche's (1844–1900) Übermensch, literally a "super man." They're not identical, but both the Übermensch and the sovereign are trailblazers who detest being beholden to anyone and refuse to be tethered by other people's cultural or moral traditions.

Cosmic Battle of Ideals

These two masculine ideals are magnified through the archangels Michael and Lucifer. Michael is the ultimate warrior of Heaven, the epitome of an obedient soldier and son. As Michael's vessel, Dean is the human equivalent of Michael's masculinity. In fact, Michael embodies many virtues that Dean strives to attain throughout the series. On the flip side, Lucifer is a bit more complicated. Sam doesn't explicitly strive to be like Lucifer, although Lucifer does try to convince Sam that they're exactly alike. Of course, there are certainly some striking similarities. For example, Lucifer, the prodigal son, refuses to blindly obey his father, preferring to think freely as sovereign in Hell.

Season 5 and the approach of the Apocalypse depict a clash between a son's duty as a soldier and an individual's freedom of thought and will. Michael and Lucifer constantly criticize each other for not seeing things from the other's perspective. The season finale reveals that this feud is based on an overly simplistic understanding of their two masculine ideals. Meanwhile Sam and Dean demonstrate that adopting aspects of both the warrior and the sovereign make them better hunters and people. This is further highlighted when the angels, Castiel and Anna, realize that an angel's unwillingness to deviate from an absolute makes them inferior to humanity with its ability to combine conflicting ideals.

The Dirty Word in *Supernatural*, the L-Word

DEAN: You're supposed to say "jerk."

Considering that the show is about a family of hunters who repeatedly die and go to Hell for each other, it's striking that almost no one talks about "love." Sam and Dean will talk for days about sacrifice, devotion, trust, protecting one another, and dying for one another, but when the conversation turns from actions to emotions, the brothers are silent.[3]

Scenes with Sam, Dean, and Bobby are practically competitions for disguising their emotions. They stoically resist all urges to open up about their feelings, belittling anyone the moment they do. This ends when one of them finally admits that being emotionally spent or rage-filled makes them poor hunters and people. But no doubt, they soon forget. This dysfunction is very clear to people outside this inner circle of stoics. In Season 1, Dean's ex-girlfriend Cassie notes, "I forgot you do that. Whenever we get close—anywhere in the vicinity of emotional vulnerability—you back off." And yet, even when the characters learn this lesson time and again, they rarely seem any closer to explicitly expressing affection, let alone grappling with the L-word.

Finally, though, in Season 5, we get the moment we've all been waiting for—the brothers talk about the love they have for family. Sam even goes so far as to tell Dean he loves him, although he was severely doped up at the time. Clearly, the love is there, but the brothers have serious inhibitions when it comes to expressing it. Given the persistent lack of love-talk in the show, the episode "Abandon All Hope," is ironically a nexus for love, hunting, and masculinity. Ellen, holding her dying daughter in her arms, says, "I will always love you, baby." This is the first time we've ever heard a hunter explicitly express love for a family member they weren't married to.

Ellen's last words to Jo are a foil for the brothers' feelings. Shortly after leaving Ellen and Jo to face their fate, Sam and Dean are forced to confront the fact that they will probably die as well. Even in this moment, considering what their last words should be, Sam and Dean just can't bring themselves to say what a mother so effortlessly could.

Supernatural on Femininity: Less Than Admiration

BEN: Only bitches send a grownup.

Supernatural is largely about men navigating their masculinity, but you can't really talk about masculinity without simultaneously commenting on femininity. The characters and the show itself appear to have some vacillating opinions of women and femininity. For instance, when Jo accuses Dean of being sexist in "No Exit," he retorts, "Sweetheart, this ain't gender studies. Women can do the job fine. Amateurs can't." Clearly, though, Dean knows nothing about gender studies, since his future actions fail to live up to these words. Dean claims that he thinks women can "do the job fine," but he never misses an opportunity to insult Sam for getting beat by a woman. Contrast that with the fact that Dean and Sam never make fun of each other for getting beat up by amateurs. In fact, if you look at the teasing between the brothers (and even Bobby) a disturbing amount of it relies on implying that one of them is acting like a woman. The same can't be said for acting like an amateur. So when Dean tells Jo that he has no issues with women being capable fighters, Jo appropriately gives him some heavy side eye. If Dean didn't really associate women with weakness, he wouldn't have smiled approvingly in "The Kids Are Alright" when Ben, says, "only bitches send a grown-up."

There's another issue, however, that goes beyond the unintentional sexism of Sam and Dean. Several women in the show directly challenge Sam and Dean's chivalric tendencies and ideals of masculinity. Jo, Sarah, and Lisa all suggest that the boys' desire to protect the women they care about is not entirely praiseworthy, thus challenging the core notion that a warrior should use his strength to protect others. The show provides foil on top of foil—Castiel, Uriel, Adam, Michael, Lucifer, Bobby, Andy, and Ansem—to explore every possible argument regarding whether men should try to protect and save one another, but the show provides almost nothing to explore human women who want to do the saving. In nearly every case of women actively protecting their families, they've been monsters or demons. The only exceptions are Mary, Jo, and Ellen. But, keep in mind that Jo's "an amateur," Ellen doesn't want to be a hunter, and Mary has been mostly dead since the first episode.

While the boys have struggled with whether their protection of one another is helpful or hurtful, the show has remained practically silent on whether this uncertainty extends to the women in their lives. They regularly whine about not having protected their mother or Jess or some other important woman in their life, but they never seem to wonder whether their warrior ideal is at times an overblown savior complex.

Erotically Co-Dependent?

ZACHARIAH: Sam and Dean Winchester are psychotically, irrationally, erotically codependent on each other.

There are lots of jokes about sexuality in *Supernatural*, and many of them are cheap jibes about how embarrassing it is for straight men to be perceived as gay. But in the midst of all this encouragement to chuckle along with Sam and Dean's homophobia, we also get some humorous moments that call for serious reflection on how hetero-sexuality and masculinity can influence one another. For example, in Season 5, Sam and Dean attend a gathering for *Supernatural* fans where there is a panel discussion on "The Homoerotic Subtext of *Supernatural*." At first, this seems to be a crude joke. We laugh, because it's funny to think about how embarrassed Sam and Dean must feel, hearing this. But the homoerotic subtext sets up a beautiful irony for the episode's conclusion. After meeting devoted fans, Demian and Barnes, who are LARPing as the brothers, Dean com-plains that emulating the Winchesters is idiotic, because their life "sucks." Without missing a beat, Demian responds:

> I'm not sure you get what the [*Supernatural*] stories are about ... In real life, he sells stereo equipment. I fix copiers. Our lives suck. But to be Sam and Dean, to wake up every morning and save the world. To have a brother who would die for you. Well who wouldn't want that?

Again, the L-word isn't used here. But Demian and Barnes pretend to be Sam and Dean because they like being able to partake in the brotherly love between them. The twist, of course, occurs when Sam and Dean realize that, on top of being friends, Demian and Barnes are also a couple. Their nerdy, cheesy fandom then becomes a reflec-tion on the similarities between brotherly love and romantic love.

Supernatural's fan service is certainly not the first attempt to make this connection. Comparing and contrasting familial love, friendship, and erotic love was a well-trodden pastime of several ancient Greek philosophers as well. For instance, in Plato's (427 BCE–347 BCE) dialogue *The Symposium* the playwright Aristophanes (446 BCE–386 BCE) recounts a myth about how everyone once shared a body with their soulmate. Some of these soulmate pairs were men and women, but others were two women or two men. When Zeus sundered all the ball-shaped soulmates into two separate people, everyone started running around trying to find their other half. While soulmates are often thought of as being sexual partners (Aristophanes noted that it was odd how these soulmated people wanted to spend all their time together—and not just because of the great sex), people also exhibit this kind of behavior in other relationships. Sam and Dean spend all their time together, and they seem to genuinely enjoy each other's company.

When other characters mistake Sam and Dean for a couple, this is not just a crude attempt at homophobic humor. It also reflects that many Americans are not used to observing intimacy in people unless they're romantic partners. We joke about "bromances," because we struggle with the idea that men—emotionally stoic and self-sufficient creatures—can engage in tender and intimate relations with one another, especially if they are straight. Even if we think we're okay with the idea of men having sex with other men, we still may have the impulse to laugh at two men being caring and intimate friends. This tension comes out when the angel Zachariah yells in a fit of frustration that Sam and Dean are "psychotically, irrationally, erotically codependent on each other." Their intimacy and personal devotion to one another seems so deviant that it looks like a mental illness (or sexual tension) to Zachariah.[4]

Sam and Dean's relationship wouldn't have looked quite as weird to Aristotle (384 BCE–322 BCE), though. Sure, the demons would have given him pause, but Aristotle argued that some of the purest love to be had is that between friends, particularly, that between two virtuous men. There are lots of reasons to suspect that Sam and Dean wouldn't have fit Aristotle's bill for being virtuous, but they do fit his insistence that two men can share a bond of such great strength and intimacy that we can really only call it "love."

The Paradox of Love in *Supernatural*

DEAN: The point is … maybe we are each other's Achilles heel […] I don't know. I just know we're all we've got. More than that. We keep each other human.

Love is a paradox in *Supernatural* with its masculine ideals of strength and independence. But in order to be masculine, one must first and foremost be human. And to be human, one needs love. Thus, masculinity needs to embrace something it has not traditionally prioritized—something that does not come "naturally" to it. To be fully human then, Sam and Dean must embrace what is seemingly supernatural: love.

Notes

1. The episode "What Is and What Should Never Be" (Season 2, Episode 20) is a good place to see this. Not only does Dean say "bitch" with a smile, but he also looks disappointed when Sam does not respond with his normal come back.
2. If you look at American pop culture, for instance, the singers Beyoncé and Christina Aguilera—who are held up as two icons of femininity—have songs specifically about strength and independence ("Independent Women Part I": http://tinyurl.com/2ajvum3; "Fighter": http://tinyurl.com/yd3soyw, accessed March 19, 2013).
3. Dean has directly told his mother he loves her (Season 5, Episode 16). He has spoken of his father loving Sam. He has told Sam's corpse, "I guess that's what I do; let down the people I love" (Season 2, Episode 22). He even once said to Sam, "Whatever we have between us, love, family, they will use that against us" (Season 5, Episode 4). Sam, once, while doped up on medication, told Dean, "You're my brother and I still love you" (Season 5, Episode 11). He has also spoken of his father to somebody else, "I love him" (Season 5, Episode 13). And Bobby has commented to Dean, "Maybe we love him [Sam] too much" (Season 4, Episode 20). Notice, almost all of these invocations of the L-word happen in Season 5, which means there were a full four seasons of Sam and Dean (and their father, and Bobby) not even using the word in each other's presence more than once or twice.
4. To some degree, it is a valid question whether Sam and Dean are unhealthily codependent on one another. But the addition of "erotically" in Zachariah's outburst reveals that part of the reason Sam and Dean's relationship seems so "weird" is because it's what we expect of lovers, not brothers.

Chapter 15

Naturalizing *Supernatural*

Joseph L. Graves, Jr.

Would you have predicted that Eve could be killed with the ash of a phoenix? Does it make sense that ghosts and demons have issues crossing lines of salt, or that burning the bones of either destroys them? Did you expect Lucifer would be able to obliterate so many lesser gods without making much effort? The Colt—how does that thing work, and what are the five things it can't kill? And why doesn't it work on archangels? Ultimately, the key to unraveling many, but not all, of these questions is taking a systematic approach to understanding the universe, commonly attributed to naturalists.

The *Supernatural* universe consists of both supernatural and natural beings and elements. The supernatural beings include God, archangels, minor gods, leviathans, angels, reapers, demons, and spirits. The natural beings are humans and other organic life. Monsters such as vampires, werewolves, and shapeshifters seem to have both natural and supernatural features. Important elements from the show range from the purely supernatural objects like Angel Swords, to natural objects with supernatural features like the Colt or holy water, and finally to purely natural objects like iron, salt, blood, and herbs, that have power over supernatural beings. In line with the blending of the supernatural and the natural, life in the *Supernatural* world results from special creation along with organic

Supernatural and Philosophy: Metaphysics and Monsters ... for Idjits, First Edition.
Edited by Galen A. Foresman.
© 2013 John Wiley & Sons, Inc. Published 2013 by John Wiley & Sons, Inc.

evolution. Castiel captures this in a poignant comment from "The Man Who Would Be King":

> I remember being at a shoreline, watching a little grey fish heave itself up on the beach. And an older brother saying, "Don't step on that fish, Castiel, big plans for that fish." I remember the Tower of Babel—all 37 feet of it, which I suppose was impressive at the time. And when it fell they howled, "Divine Wrath!" But come on, dried dung can only be stacked so high.

So the natural and the supernatural are there together from the beginning in *Supernatural*, even though most present-day characters aren't fully aware of the supernatural. As hunters, Sam and Dean Winchester are exceptions. They have specialized knowledge and they use both natural and supernatural means to save people and hunt things. The fact that the Winchesters are able to blend their knowledge of the supernatural with the natural suggests that understanding the supernatural world may not be as difficult as prophets reading tablets lead us to believe.

At some points in the show, we are left believing that the supernatural has supremacy over the natural, as is reflected in the quote from Castiel. At other times, we see the utility of the natural when aligned against the supernatural, which is often demonstrated through the actions and lives of the Winchester brothers. This interplay in *Supernatural* suggests that there are some rules regarding the relationships between the supernatural world and the natural world. Rules are helpful, of course, since they allow us to make predictions about the future. If we could understand, for example, how the Colt was made, we could see how it would be possible for Sam and Dean to create an entire armory of useful weapons.

What Do a Naturalist and a Supernaturalist Have in Common?

The supernatural includes any phenomenon or entity that operates outside of natural processes, but that doesn't necessarily mean that they operate *entirely* outside of these processes. So, for example,

Jesus walking along the surface of the Sea of Galilee in Mark 6:45–52 would be supernatural since we cannot explain how a man could do this using scientific knowledge of natural processes. Natural processes, by contrast, are those processes that can be entirely observed or understood via the five human senses or their extensions in the material world. These observations in tandem with the scientific method are our primary means for understanding the natural world. So, for example, a water strider insect walking along the surface tension of water would be natural, because, given our knowledge of the chemistry of surface tension, we can understand this phenomenon in terms of natural processes. We cannot, however, use the same knowledge of chemistry to explain a man walking along the Sea of Galilee, which mixes something perfectly natural, a man, and a phenomenon that is outside of natural processes. Similarly, since *Supernatural* blends natural and supernatural processes, we can probably, to a limited extent, use scientific thinking to better understand rules guiding the interaction between the two worlds, even some that help us to better understand the supernatural world.

Naturalism posits that natural phenomena are explained by other natural phenomena. Thus, a naturalist would not credit a spirit with the disappearance of a water spill on the kitchen floor but rather would explain it in terms of evaporation. Naturalism is the philosophical basis that drove the development of the scientific method, a process for obtaining knowledge that tests hypotheses through experiments and attempts to generate universal rules that govern the behavior of phenomena.

To see the differences between naturalist thinking and supernaturalist thinking, compare these two possible explanations of a mental illness. A naturalist explanation would use neurobiology to explain mental illness as driven by brain anomalies either in structure or chemistry. By contrast, a supernatural explanation of mental illness might involve the possession of the person by an evil spirit or demon. Both of these explanations are rule driven, but the rules differ in how they may be tested. A battery of mental, anatomical, and chemical tests can be given to detect brain malfunction. Indeed, the Catholic Church considers organic mental illness as its first explanation before considering granting a rite of exorcism. In other words, the Catholic Church first assumes a naturalistic explanation for mental illness before resorting to a supernaturalistic explanation.

Like the Catholic Church, we will also first assume a naturalist explanation for phenomena in *Supernatural* and posit a hypothesis in naturalistic terms. Where naturalism fails to account for all the supernatural phenomena, we can always blame it on currently inadequate data (giving us all the excuse we need to watch more episodes).

The War in Heaven and Naturally Averting God's Plan

In *Supernatural*, the Judeo-Christian god is presented as the most powerful being in the universe. But did he create all things? If so, then how do we account for pagan gods, like Kali, Thor, and others? In "Hammer of the Gods" many of these gods claim they existed before the Judeo-Christian god, and therefore, have the right to prevent the Judeo-Christian Apocalypse. In terms of what we know as naturalists, we can draw a few conclusions from this. Assuming the pagan gods were telling the truth, in that they existed before the Judeo-Christian god, then they could not have been created by that god. However, their claimed right to prevent the Apocalypse does not follow simply from their existing first. As many of us learned in pre-school, just because someone or something is older, doesn't make it the boss of the universe.

Apart from this and a few other references to a time before the creation of the angels and archangels, most of the supernatural phenomena from the show come through the central plot device of seasons 1 through 5. The primary story arch for these seasons is based on Judeo-Christian lore and the "war in Heaven." This war is alluded to in Ezechiel 28:1–19, Isaiah 14:12–15, Luke 10:18; 2 Peter 2:4, Jude 6; and Revelation 12:3–4, 7–9; and also in the apocryphal texts of Enoch 1 and 2. This war is central to Christian theology, in that it plays a key role in explaining how both evil and humans come into the world. After all, if God is all-powerful, all-knowing, and all-good, how could he have created a world in which so much evil and misery prevails? Of course, naturalists have an easy time answering this question, since they can simply deny the existence of the supernatural, claiming instead that it was we who created "God" precisely to give a rationale for our own evil acts. But for those who accept the existence of God, the existence of evil is a bit of a puzzle.

Sam and Dean Winchester struggle throughout the series with whether God and his angels are "good," which often leads them to question whether a supernatural design is better than a natural plan of action. Indeed, in Season 2 we find Dean Winchester still unconvinced that God and angels exist. The brothers only come to truly believe in angels after they meet Castiel in Season 4. Yet despite their knowledge of the existence of angels, Heaven, and God, they insist on circumventing God's plan. Their defiance seems to indicate that they think their reason, which is derived from a natural structure, the brain, is superior to the supernatural design of God.

The Soul: Supernatural Genetic Code

Due to the fact that organisms are self-replicating, and replication cannot be perfect in the material world, genetic codes must evolve. This fact is recognized in the universe of *Supernatural* as Castiel recounts being on hand to watch the proto-tetrapod ancestor of humans crawling out of a Paleozoic sea to begin colonization of the land. This recognition runs in parallel to the war in Heaven supernatural narrative, in which souls are analogous to the genetic codes of the natural world. A naturalist could hypothesize that souls self-replicate through the very same biological process that delivers all our children, since whenever we replicate we tend to also increase the total number of souls. This would make souls far less supernatural than we might have initially thought.

In "Appointment at Samarra," Death tells Dean Winchester, "The human soul is not a rubber ball. It is vulnerable, impermanent, but stronger than you know. And more valuable than you can imagine."

We see more evidence of this in "My Heart Will Go On," when we learn that the angel Baltazar creates an alternative time line by preventing the sinking of the Titanic. As a result, 50,000 individuals are born who would have otherwise not existed. This provides us further evidence for our naturalistic account of soul creation. Atropos tells Castiel that she knows why he ordered Baltazar to take that action, "50,000 souls for his war machine …" Here, *Supernatural* blends the naturalistic creation of souls with the supernatural war in Heaven narrative.

In later episodes, the war in Heaven narrative lends support for a naturalist explanation for the souls in Purgatory. In "The Man Who Would Be King," we learn that Castiel had made a deal with Crowley to split the souls in Purgatory, the power of which he planned to use to win his war in Heaven against the archangel Rafael. And in "The Man Who Knew Too Much," Castiel consumes all the souls of Purgatory, destroys Rafael, and declares himself the new "God." From this bit of story line, we know there are souls in Purgatory, not unlike our own, in that they possess great power, and they can be wielded and manipulated by angels and demons. If these souls originated on Earth, we'd have our rule-guided explanation for all these similarities.

In fact, there is some evidence that all beings in the *Supernatural* universe have souls, possibly even God. Of course, God's having a soul would mean that not all souls originate through humanity's biological process. For now, at least, this is a question left needing more research data. In "Two Minutes to Midnight," Death explains to Dean how insignificant he and the planet Earth are to him, "This is a little planet, in a tiny solar system, in a galaxy that is barely out of its diapers." Death further explains to Dean that he is as old as God, possibly older, although he can't quite remember. Apparently, age impacts the supernatural memory in much the same ways it impacts our natural memories. In this conversation, Death equates God with life, suggesting that both exist in a near-eternal cosmic duality. In addition, Death claims that "At the end I will reap him too. God will die too, Dean."

But what happens to Death once God has been reaped? If God is life and Death is, well, death, then with no more life, there could be no more death. Could this be an allusion to the end of all existence? Could this be a claim that God and Death are indeed natural products themselves, since all life begins and ends with them?

The relationship between the supernatural and natural is illustrated in both the creation of entities and how they can be destroyed. Like our natural biological process for creating souls, how an entity can be destroyed tells us how closely it's tied to naturalistic rules and explanations. Beginning with our recently hypothesized duality of God and Death, they are the ultimate cause for existence. This is followed by the war in Heaven narrative—God created archangels, angels, humans, and all other organic, sapient, and souled beings in the universe. The fallen angels, led by Lucifer, created demons from human souls. In Season 6, we learn that "Eve" is the mother of all monsters, and she's older than angels. Eve controls Purgatory, the place that monsters go when they are destroyed in the natural universe.

Like demons, monsters may also find the original creation of their souls tied to human souls, since a great many of them are converted to monster from a human state. In some cases, we simply don't have enough evidence to speak categorically for all monsters, but for vampires, werewolves, rugaru, shapeshifters, and wendigo, it's safe to say that all but the Alphas began as humans. This hypothesis would help explain why these monsters are vulnerable to very natural objects, like silver and sharp knives. Even the development of Eve's most recent monster, the "Jefferson Starships," required several experimental trials on humans before getting this hybrid just right. The end result was a "horrible and hard to kill" monster susceptible to run-of-the-mill decapitation.

In "Hammer of the Gods" Lucifer makes short work of the pagan gods gathered to prevent the Judeo-Christian Apocalypse, demonstrating that the pagan gods are inferior to the fallen angels. We also know that the pagan gods are vulnerable to natural objects. Hol Nekar and his wife were killed with a pine stake; Leshii was decapitated; Veritas was killed with a blade dipped in dog's blood; and Chronos was similarly killed with an ancient olive stake dipped in some sort of blood. The fact that natural objects had power over pagan gods suggests that these entities were not really gods, but more akin to monsters. Furthermore, the fact that these "gods" required humans for their survival suggests that they were created some time after humans, either that or they were very hungry up until humans were created.

Ultimately, Eve ingests the ash of another monster, the phoenix, and is destroyed. This makes her different from Lucifer or God, since neither the chief fallen angel nor God are vulnerable to materials or entities that are lower on the scale of being than they are. Regardless, if God and Eve always existed, then they could themselves be "natural," but just obeying laws of nature not shared by lesser natural beings, like ourselves. If this were true, they might believe in their own divinity simply because they are unaware of any existence before their own. Of note, however, is the fact that Purgatory was created by God to hold an early creation, the leviathans, which predated the angels and the soul. The Alpha-Vampire suggests in "There Will Be Blood" that Eve was a leviathan, which would ultimately make her another one of God's creations. In addition to monsters and demigods, natural objects and processes have power over spirits. In the *Supernatural* phylogeny, ghosts arise from humans. According to the "rules," spirits are supposed to accompany reapers after death to either Heaven or Hell. Spirits become ghosts when they refuse to leave this plane, usually due to some violent death or unfinished business. Some of these spirits may become demons, either through a deal made in life with a demon, or possibly via a metamorphosis triggered by their own immoral acts during life.

Given that demons and spirits share a source of creation in the human soul, it makes sense that they'd be vulnerable to some of the same natural objects. Both ghosts and demons cannot cross salt lines, and the destruction of their human remains (bones, hair) by salt and fire destroys them. Indeed, we learn that Crowley, the King of Hell, is a metamorphosed human soul and he is, therefore, vulnerable to destruction via the burning of his bones. Thus, Crowley is a poor substitute for Lucifer, who was never human, and therefore has no mundane vulnerabilities.

In addition to these purely natural means for destroying supernatural entities, there are also natural objects infused with supernatural powers that work as well. Samuel Colt's pistol is a special version of his colt revolver, along with special bullets, that could kill virtually any entity in creation. Only archangels appear to be immune. The source of the magic involved in the manufacture of this weapon is never revealed. Similarly, holy water is just water that has been blessed, but it manages to burn demons in a way that normal water doesn't. Unfortunately, it does not destroy them. Demons, on the other hand, can be sent back to Hell via the rite of exorcism, recited in Latin, and they can be imprisoned via the Seal of Solomon. Clearly, this rite and seal must derive their power from Heaven.

Conversely, the magic used by witches and cursed objects derive their power from Hell. Additional natural objects infused with demonic supernatural power are demon blood and the Croatoan virus. Demon blood is human blood resulting from a demon possessing a human, and the Croatoan virus is a virus infused with some demonic supernatural energy that creates homicidal madness in the infected person. Sam becomes addicted to demon blood during Season 4, and his ingestion of demon blood magnifies his psychic powers, allowing him to mentally exorcise demons. Lucifer's plan for the destruction of the human species involved the mass infection of humanity with Croatoan virus, but it is unclear whether Croatoan virus is entirely supernatural, or whether it is a natural virus, infused with demonic properties. The latter case seems to be more likely, given that in "Two Minutes to Midnight," we see that the Croatoan virus was manufactured by Niveus Pharmaceuticals.

These connections between the natural and the supernatural help explain how objects and entities interact throughout *Supernatural*. But importantly, they also support story points. For example, Lucifer's plan to destroy all of humanity proves that he not only dislikes humans, but he cares very little for anything derived from a human soul. By destroying mankind, he would have prevented any future production of demons, and he would have starved the world of Eve's monsters. While not entirely perfect, an attempted naturalistic explanation helps tie the world of the supernatural together and makes for a far richer world in *Supernatural*.

Naturally All Part of the Plan

The actions of Sam and Dean Winchester, a motley crew of hunters, and a couple of rebellious angels short-circuit the prophesized Christian Apocalypse. We are of course left wondering how this could have happened, especially if God is the most powerful being in this universe. Fortunately, we now know that answers to questions like these aren't beyond our reach. We've used our very natural brain to reason through some of the trickier questions posed by *Supernatural*. And even though we didn't satisfactorily answer all our inquiries—leaving us to keep wondering how the Colt works, and what can't it kill—at least we've discovered through the lens of a naturalist that many supernatural entities and objects in *Supernatural* are limited by some fairly ordinary thinking about natural phenomena. In which case, averting the prophesied Christian Apocalypse may just have been another sign from God that it's time to move away from the war in Heaven supernatural narrative and on to something a little more natural.

Clearly, the naturalism in *Supernatural* suggests that he did have "big plans for that little grey fish."

Contributors
Bona Fide, Card Carrying Wisdom Lovers and GhostPhacers

Carey F. Applegate, Ph.D., is an Assistant Professor of English at the University of Wisconsin–Eau Claire, where she teaches courses in English education, composition, and (pop) cultural studies. She researches and writes about contemporary television, film, and music; twenty-first-century pedagogy; and digital grassroots advocacy. Her free time in the summer is spent LARPing with Charlie Bradbury and noshing on pie with Dean Winchester, while her winters usually involve the search for a portal to an alternative, non-snowy, *Doctor Who*/*Supernatural*-mashup reality. If you'd like to participate in her adventures, drop her a note on Twitter: @careyapplegate.

James Blackmon teaches philosophy at San Francisco State University. He's not as cool as Sam or Dean, but some of his notebooks are almost as cool as John's journal. Despite having accumulated a few personal episodes which would count as anecdotal evidence in favor of ghosts and demons, he still doesn't believe in them. This skepticism, of course, surely pleases some ghosts and demons to no end.

Patricia Brace, Ph.D., is a Professor of Art at Southwest Minnesota State University in Marshall, Minnesota. Her research interests are

Supernatural and Philosophy: Metaphysics and Monsters ... for Idjits, First Edition.
Edited by Galen A. Foresman.
© 2013 John Wiley & Sons, Inc. Published 2013 by John Wiley & Sons, Inc.

in aesthetics and popular culture and she has written chapters for *Dexter and Philosophy* (2011), and *The Philosophy of Joss Whedon* (2011). She also studies and teaches a course on the history of jewelry and her creative artistic work is in jewelry design. In that capacity she was commissioned to fashion amulets and talismans for the reclusive owner of a junkyard in nearby Sioux Falls, South Dakota, Mr. Bobby Singer. She was saddened to hear about Mr. Singer's recent death from his colleague, a rather odd little man who identified himself only as "Garth" and put in an order for Mandaic amulets, silver ampullae for holy water, and brandea pendants for Oil of Abramelin.

John Edgar Browning is an Arthur A. Schomburg Fellow and Ph.D. student in American studies at the University at Buffalo (SUNY) where he also teaches on the adjunct English Faculty. He has co-/edited and co-/written ten published and forthcoming books, including *Draculas, Vampires, and Other Undead Forms: Essays on Gender, Race, and Culture* (2009), *Dracula in Visual Media: Film, Television, Comic Book and Electronic Game Appearances, 1921–2010* (2010), *The Vampire, His Kith and Kin: A Critical Edition* (2011), *Speaking of Monsters: A Teratological Anthology* (2012), and *The Forgotten Writings of Bram Stoker* (2012). He has also co-/written chapters for *Asian Gothic: Essays on Literature, Film, and Anime* (2008), *The Encyclopedia of the Vampire: The Living Dead in Myth, Legend, and Popular Culture* (2010), *Nyx in the House of Night: Mythology, Folklore, and Religion in the PC and Kristin Cast Vampyre Series* (2011), *Fear and Learning: Essays on the Pedagogy of Horror* (forthcoming 2013), *Undead in the West 2: They Just Keep Coming* (forthcoming 2013), *The Encyclopedia of the Zombie: The Walking Dead in Popular Culture and Myth* (forthcoming 2013), and *A Companion to the Horror Film* (Wiley-Blackwell, forthcoming 2014). When he isn't writing about vampires, he's studying them in the wilds of New Orleans and Buffalo. He also likes to far exceed his bio word count limit.

Jillian L. Canode received her Ph.D. in philosophy and literature from Purdue University in 2011. Her current research interests lie in exploring the ethical and political landscapes of identity and self-definition in and through social media. As a self-professed Dean-girl and long-time supporter of Team Free Will, Dr. Canode spends her free time brushing up on her Enochian so as not to bring upon herself the wrath of the nerd angels.

Danilo Chaib wrote his thesis on conductorless orchestras at the Equality Studies with the School of Social Justice at the University College Dublin. His career began in 1997 when he was saved by John Winchester from a demon-possessed conductor. Ever since, Danilo has confused demons and conductors, ferociously hunting them as John did. In his free time, he teaches chamber music, philosophy of music, and research in music education at the Escola de Música de Brasília, Brazil. He is currently working on his second doctoral research with the University of Granada, Spain. His mission to wipe conductors from the orchestral world continues (much to the chagrin of many successful orchestras).

Fredrick Curry, or at least his "on grid" identity, earned his Ph.D. in philosophy at Bowling Green State University Ohio and his BA in English from California State University Fullerton. He loves teaching, is an avid gamer, and enjoys computer programming as a hobby. He currently teaches at WVU, where he most definitely isn't part of a secret society of Letters, or busy designing demon-trap laser pointers and rub-on angelic glyph tattoos.

Shannon B. Ford, MA, is a Research Associate and Doctoral Candidate with the Centre for Applied Philosophy and Public Ethics (CAPPE) and Adjunct Lecturer with the Australian Graduate School of Policing and Security, Charles Sturt University. Before starting a full-time academic career, Shannon spent ten years in the Department of Defense as a Strategist and Intelligence Analyst. During that time, he never personally investigated any "mysterious" deaths characterized by significant amounts of blood splatter on the walls. But he does have a closet full of sharp suits and a notepad, just in case. His research interests include: police, military and intelligence ethics; the correlation between driving a '67 Chevy Impala, listening to AC/DC and awesomeness; and TV shows involving monster-hunting mysteries, Timelords, or a spy who once fought the Evil Dead.

Galen A. Foresman, Ph.D., is an Assistant Professor in Philosophy at North Carolina A&T State University. He spends half his time teaching, half his time researching, and half his time with family and friends. He recently won the title "Assessment Genius" from the Center of Inquiry in the Liberal Arts, which was later robbed from him by an "Assessment Ninja." In preparation for editing this book he watched every episode of *Supernatural* in the space of three days, which really isn't impossible if you think about it. His current claim to fame is editing this book, and he got loads of help from personal friends Dr. Badass and Mr. Fizzles.

Stacey Goguen studies philosophy at Boston University, where she works on implicit bias, philosophy of race, and feminist philosophy. She just happens to be one of the five things in all of creation that the Colt cannot kill.

Joseph L. Graves, Jr. is Associate Dean for Research & Professor of Biological Sciences, Joint School of Nanosciences and Nanoengineering. He received his Ph.D. in environmental, evolutionary and systematic biology from Wayne State University in 1988. In 1994 he was elected a Fellow of the Council of the American Association for the Advancement of Science (AAAS). His current research involves the genomics of adaptation, specifically relevant to aging, as well as the theory and methods of computational evolutionary phylogenetics and molecular evolution. His books on the biology of race are entitled: *The Emperor's New Clothes: Biological Theories of Race at the Millennium* (2001, 2005) and *The Race Myth: Why We Pretend Race Exists in America* (2004, 2005). His main hobbies include the dispatching of demons and monsters, particularly vampires who use *Twilight* hysteria to prey upon middle-aged housewives.

Daniel Haas, Ph.D., absolutely did not bury a lunch box at the crossroad a mile out of town. And that lunch box, which Dan never buried, absolutely did not contain a personal photo, dirt from the local graveyard, or a black cat bone. Why would you bury that stuff in a lunch box anyways? And he's never seen a demon, let alone kissed one. Nope. Never ever. He earned all those degrees all on his own. Pure natural talent. That's all it was. Did you hear that barking? Yeah, me neither. No barking or scratching at the door.

Dena Hurst, Ph.D., is an instructor and researcher at Florida State University. She has doctorate in philosophy, with a specialization in social and political philosophy, and a bachelor's degree in economics. Her current research interests include the philosophy of race, class, and gender, models of power, radical philosophy, and popular culture. Her work includes working with government agencies on issues of governance, leadership, and ethics. For a short while, following the sudden death of Ash, the Winchesters relied on her master research skills, until they began to suspect that, like most radical philosophers, her sympathies were with the wrong side.

Devon Fitzgerald Ralston, Ph.D., is a Visiting Assistant Professor at Miami University in Oxford, Ohio, where she teaches composition, professional writing, and cultural studies courses. She focuses her research and writing efforts on social media and identity, as well as *Frankenstein* and early sci-fi texts. Her current project examines the ways in which digital craft blogs transform both the narrative of community as well as the particular craft itself. She collects robot kitsch and vintage film posters, often wondering if she is stuck in one of the trickster's time loops before realizing that no, those are still the same stack of student papers as before. Or are they?

Nathan Stout is a Ph.D. candidate in the philosophy department at Tulane University. His LSAT score of 174 would have earned him a full ride at Stanford Law had it not been discovered that he falsified his application materials by applying under the pseudonym,

"Mr. Jimmy Page." He now spends his time studying moral philosophy with a focus on problems in responsibility, agency, and political violence. Despite his best efforts, and the fact that he lives in New Orleans, he has yet to find a single hoodoo priestess capable of laying even the slightest bit of mojo on him.

Francis Tobienne, Jr. is a Purdue Doctoral and Dali Research Fellow teaching classes on monsters, the occult tradition, and the *Bible* as occult literature at the University of South Florida, St. Petersburg campus. He is the author of *The Position of Magic in Selected Medieval Spanish Texts* (2008). He is currently working on two monographs: "Dali's Medievalism" and "Mandeville's Travels." Dr. Tobienne publishes widely in the fields of medieval studies, pop culture, intellectual history, and medical ethics. He is currently working tirelessly on how to get Castiel to grow a full-on beard for crying out loud! Why? Because God commanded it.

Index

Supernatural and Philosophy: Metaphysics and Monsters... for Idjits, First Edition.
Edited by Galen A. Foresman.
© 2013 John Wiley & Sons, Inc. Published 2013 by John Wiley & Sons, Inc.

Printed and bound by CPI Group (UK) Ltd, Croydon, CR0 4YY

25/03/2025

14647357-0002